Contemporary Arab Broadcast Media

Contemporary Arab Broadcast Media

EL MUSTAPHA LAHLALI

EDINBURGH UNIVERSITY PRESS

© El Mustapha Lahlali, 2011

Edinburgh University Press Ltd
22 George Square, Edinburgh
www.euppublishing.com

Typeset in Linotype Palatino
by Iolaire Typesetting, Newtonmore and
printed and bound in Great Britain by
CPI Antony Rowe, Chippenham and Eastbourne

A CIP record for this book is available from the British Library

ISBN 978 0 7486 3909 0 (hardback)
ISBN 978 0 7486 3908 3 (paperback)

Contents

Acknowledgements

I would like to express my gratitude to all those who made this book possible. I wish to thank first and foremost my colleagues in the department of Arabic and Middle Eastern Studies, University of Leeds, for their support and encouragement. My special thanks go to James Dale and Nicola Ramsey, Edinburgh University Press, for supporting this project.

My special thanks are due to employees in Al-Jazeera, Al-Hurra and Al-Arabiya for answering my questions and responding to my enquiries.

My heartfelt appreciation also goes to all my friends for their support, help and encouragement. Special thanks go to my friend, Mohamed Rachidi, for his encouragement throughout the writing stages of this book. I am also obliged to my nephews and nieces for their enthusiastic questions about this project.

Lastly, and most importantly, I would like to express my warm thanks to my parents, brothers and sisters for their unfailing love, encouragement and support.

Introduction

Before the war on Afghanistan in 2001, Arab media was almost unheard of; however, Al-Jazeera's monopoly over the coverage of the war on Afghanistan has put Arab media on the map. While some people have struggled to grasp the reasons behind the long silence of the Arab media, others have shown a positive attitude towards the new development of media outlets in this turbulent part of the world.

Since the independence of most of the Arab countries, the role of the media, both print and audio-visual, has been to safeguard Arabic culture and unity. This phase has witnessed tight control of the media by Arab regimes and governments. The Arab media's main focus on matters of concern to the Arab public shifted because of various historical and economic changes that hit the region. During the 1970s and 1980s, the Arab media robustly defended the Palestinian theme and called for Arab unity and solidarity with the Palestinians. The regional main themes apart, Arab media has been utilised to promote governments' domestic policies and the daily activities of governments and regimes. Media remains a potent weapon in the hands of governments to mobilise the public to support their policies.

Today, the Arab world is undergoing a radical media change, featuring the launch of satellite and cable television channels. This has ended an era of state-controlled media and given way to privatisation. The inception of Al-Jazeera, Al-Hurra and Al-Arabiya are few examples to list here. These three channels have contributed immensely to generating an open, free and transparent debate on all matters of concern to the Arab public. Although these channels broadcast in the same language, Arabic, they have different sponsors, different aims and objectives, and different ideologies.

This book aims to provide a comprehensive analysis of the broadcasting differences between these channels. What sets this book apart from other publications on Arab media is its focus on both the discursive practices of these channels and the sociological aspects that contribute to their formation. Hence, the aims and objectives of the book are as follows:

1. To provide a critical overview of the development of Arab media.
2. To examine the aims, objectives and programmes of Al-Jazeera, Al-Hurra and Al-Arabiya.
3. To examine the similarities and differences in broadcasting between these channels.
4. To examine the impact of these channels on the Arab public sphere through their discursive practices.

The aftermath of September 11th has focused global media attention on the Arab world, and has pushed the US government to think of improving and refining its image across the Arab world. The Arabic media would appear to be the perfect channel through which this goal could be achieved; however, the coverage of the war on Afghanistan and later Iraq by some Arabic channels, such as Al-Jazeera, was highly disappointing for the US government. Being discontented with Al-Jazeera's broadcasting practices, the US government launched its own channel, Al-Hurra ('the free'). The channel's mission was to win the Arab public's hearts and minds and promote freedom and democracy in the Middle East. Such a mission has proved hard to achieve, as other Arabic channels are competing fiercely over their share of the Arab market. This stiff competition has led Arabic channels to open up to the Arab public and encourage free and democratic debate through its programmes.

This book introduces these channels to the reader in more detail. Their aims and objectives, programmes and sponsorship are discussed, compared and contrasted. Although the title of this book refers to the Arab broadcast media in general, I have chosen to focus on three Arab channels, which I believe represent the face of the Arab transnational media landscape. But before any discussion of these three channels is initiated, a historical overview is provided to acquaint the reader with the development and progress of Arab media. This historical review bears clear witness that the Arab media has moved a long way in establishing its authority and credibility as a broadcaster. It should be mentioned here, however, that the state media is still under the tight control of Arab governments. Its broadcast is still limited to domestic issues, with little focus on regional and international news.

Language as a means of communication can be very revealing indeed, not only about the producer's linguistic competence or lack thereof, but much more about the cultural, political and ideological variables that govern the production of discourse. One of the main objectives of this book is to examine the discourse practices of the three channels. I intend to look at how language reflects the channels' ideological and political views. The difference in the production of discourse or text can be very telling about the channels' main agendas. To analyse the text in relation to its social, cultural and political context, I will draw on critical discourse analysis (CDA) as a framework for that analysis. I have chosen Fairclough's framework because, as mentioned in Chapter 4, it provides us with the tools and mechanisms of dealing with the text in its wider social, cultural and political context. This particular framework is chosen because it provides a clear vision of how to link the textual analysis to the sociocultural and political analysis. This not only helps us analyse the main factors behind the production of the text, but grants us the flexibility needed to look at the text from different angles. Fairclough's framework is well known for its mechanisms of interpretation and explanation of the text. Although his framework came under a cloud of criticism for its subjective approach when analysing discourse (Widdowson 1995), I feel that his overall framework is adequate for the analysis of the coverage of the 2006 conflict between Hezbollah and Israel. Fairclough's framework differs completely from the traditional analysis of texts, which focuses mainly on the structure of sentences and the elements that constitute them. The practice was to treat sentences in isolation from each other, and the context was seen as irrelevant to the analysis of the main components constituting a sentence. The pitfalls of this type of analysis have led linguists to explore other ways of looking at sentences as a coherent entity which would help extract a coherent meaning. But despite the attempt to look at meaning across sentences, the context of the utterance of sentences remains of little importance in discovering the meaning of the text. This has changed with the emergence of discourse analysis and linguistic analysis, which have insisted on the importance of context in getting a full picture of the whole meaning. The main focus here has been on the situational and cultural context of the utterance, but the emergence of CDA has broadened the context to refer to the wider social, cultural and political context. Given the nature of the topic I am examining in this book, I believe this framework is adequate for the analysis of media discourse. Central to text production and consumption is the producer's knowledge and belief, which are often reflected in the final product.

The analysis of the data will aim to answer the following questions:

1. Do these channels use the same language and discourse in their coverage of the conflict? If not, why not?
2. What is their strategy of naming and labelling? Do they have similar attribution strategies?

By trying to answer these questions, I will be able to shed more light on the way language is used by each channel. To gain an insight into the genre of language used, I shall focus on the selectivity of lexis, naming and labelling, and the channels' use of passive and active voices. In addition to providing a textual analysis, I will provide a comprehensive analysis of the main motives behind the usage of certain aspects of language and discourse.

One of the main goals of this book is to argue the case that, in addition to the historical analysis of the development of the Arab media, the analysis of discourse can be used as a starting point to examine the ideological stance of media organisations. This type of analysis does enable us to spell out quite distinctly the main differences and similarities between different media outlets. One would envisage that because of the common language and culture, not much difference should exist between Arab channels in terms of their broadcasting; however, as evidenced by our analysis, there are some very big differences between these channels in the way they use language and impart news and information. The proliferation of satellite channels has encouraged some of these channels to adopt their own broadcasting style, without the tight control of the Arab governments over their practices. The competitive nature of this new medium has led to the production of a new discourse which varies from one channel to another. While competition remains a driving force for the variety of discourses aired to the Arab audience, globalisation is another main factor behind the changes in Arab media broadcasting. Global competition and the ability of the Arab public to access international news and information have led Arab channels to respond to this global challenge by adopting Western formats in their broadcasting. But, most importantly, these media outlets have demonstrated the ability to break away from the traditional broadcasting style of covering only local and domestic news; more time and space have been now given to regional and international affairs.

This book arose from the need to raise awareness of the different broadcasting strategies of Al-Jazeera, Al-Arabiya and Al-Hurra. In contrast to previous studies, this book, in addition to the social and ideological analysis of each channel, provides a linguistic analysis of their coverage of conflicts. The analysis highlights the way in which stories are reported and presented to the reader or viewer. While social and ideological analyses are viable options for understanding the main differences between channels, this book adds the linguistic dimension to understanding these differences.

Why Al-Jazeera, Al-Arabiya and Al-Hurra? The main impetus behind choosing these three channels is because of their representation of different views. The three channels are supported by different sponsors who play a substantial political role in the region. Moreover, because of their different objectives and strategies, these channels highlight the diversity and multiplicity of broadcasting in the region. While outlining the main similarities and differences between these channels, it is important to emphasise the historical context behind the launch of each. The Saudi government's determination to limit the hegemony of Al-Jazeera in the region is evident in their launch of Al-Arabiya as a 'moderate voice' in response to Al-Jazeera. The US government's frustration with Al-Jazeera's practice has also led to the launch of Al-Hurra, which is intended to promote freedom and democracy in the Middle East. What we have here is three different channels with completely different aims and objectives, and this is reflected in their coverage of regional and international events.

The topic of each chapter is designed to contribute to the overall theme of the book. Chapter 1 aims to provide the reader with general information about the development of the Arab media. This chapter contextualises the discussion about Al-Jazeera, Al-Arabiya and Al-Hurra. It also clearly highlights the code of practice that governs the Arab media in general.

Chapter 2 examines the impact of global media practice on the Arab media. The drastic changes on the global media stage have undeniable repercussions on the way the Arab media operates. Many countries and media organisations have launched different media outlets to reach out to the global public, which has created an atmosphere of competitiveness among the world's media. Some of this new media has been launched to counter the stereotype its culture faces; some has been launched to improve and refine their owners' image across the world; others, however, have felt that media could be used as a tool to promote their foreign policies and values.

Faced with this challenge to their own existence, some Arab governments have launched their own media to explain their policies and counter-attack other international and regional media. The fear of losing their share of the Arab media market, and their concern over the impact of the global media on the Arab public sphere has encouraged some Arab media to take strict measures to improve their practices. These measures serve as a guarantee that the Arab media is prepared to address the Arab public's concerns about the quality and independence of its broadcasting.

Chapter 3 introduces three main channels: Al-Jazeera, Al-Arabiya and Al-Hurra. A detailed analysis of the main similarities and differences between these channels is provided, with a focus on their policies, strategies, and aims and objectives. This chapter also provides the reader with an insight into the main sponsors of each channel, to help readers to form their own conclusions and opinions about each channel's practices.

Chapter 4 is devoted to the analysis of the coverage of the Israeli–Hezbollah conflict in 2006. The genre of language employed in the coverage of the conflict by these channels reveals their political and ideological orientations. The analysis shows that the channels have adopted different strategies in producing their texts/discourses. Although 'objectivity, balance and credibility' are the main ethics for producing credible news and information, these criteria are not universal among people of different cultures: different people interpret impartiality and objectivity from their own cultural perspective.

I believe this book provides an insight into the development of the Arab media and the contexts that have contributed to the proliferation of media outlets across the Arab world. This is manifested in the huge differences in the broadcasting policies between Al-Jazeera, Al-Arabiya and Al-Hurra. To demonstrate these differences, which have been compared and contrasted, I have adopted a textual analysis to pinpoint clearly the main differences in the actual production of discourse. This book not only compares and contrasts the basic tenets of the above channels, but produces a detailed analysis of their coverage of one of the most controversial conflicts in the Middle East. To produce a comprehensive and objective assessment of the coverage of the above channels, I have adopted a micro and macro analysis. I hope through this approach to give the reader a first-hand analysis of the channels' main practices. The analysis is confined to the data retrieved from the channels' websites. Some of this data is in the form of news bulletins, news articles, reports, documentaries and commentaries.

The impetus behind such an analysis, as aforementioned, is to convey to the reader the extent to which Arab media is diverse and pluralistic in its broadcasting. Through the analysis of their production of discourse, I also aim to demonstrate that objectivity and impartiality are not universals, but can vary from one channel to another. For instance, the labelling strategy used by these channels reflects their subjective views of certain groups. Although the channels cater for the same audience, their strategies and indeed their practices are different. But it should be mentioned here that the channels are aware of the risk involved when broadcasting issues not to the taste of the Arab audience. One of the central concerns of this work is to examine how the global media has created a culture of competitiveness among the Arab media. Most of the Arab media have adopted new approaches and formats in their broadcast in order to be able to compete with the highly developed Western media.

While the main emphasis of the book is on the Arab media and its broadcasting strategies, one cannot brush aside altogether the Arab public and its role in consuming this media information. The new Arab public has adopted an active role which has defined the existing relationship between it and the Arab media. The Arab public, according to Lynch (2006: 3), 'was highly self-aware of its own role in challenging the status quo, giving it a self-defined sense of mission that sometimes sat uneasily with the standards of objective journalism'. This activism has been taken seriously by transnational Arab media, which strive to win the hearts and minds of the Arab public. The new Arab public emerged with a strong Arab identity discourse reflected in the debate surrounding Arab matters. Such a debate has led to the transformation of the Arab public from being a passive agent to adopting an active role when dealing with issues of Arab interest. But it should be said here that the satellite Arab media has contributed immensely to shaping such a public. The call-in shows provided by Al-Jazeera and other channels have encouraged the Arab public to contribute to the discussion and express opinions without fear or intimidation. These platforms, along with the new media tools (such as the internet) have strengthened the Arab public's resolve and confidence in making their voices heard. Armed with technology, the Arab public started reshaping Arab political debate (Lynch 2006). This debate has resonated across the Arab world. The open space and platforms for discussion and debate have shaped Arab public opinion. The ramifications could not be ignored by the Arab regimes. The wave of demonstrations and protests in support of Palestinians across the Arab world is one example of the mobilisation of the Arab public through media.

The aftermath of September 11th could be said to have armed the Arab media with the confidence needed to questioning Arab governments' records. It has also contributed to the proliferation of media in the Arab world, especially after the war on Iraq. It goes unnoticed that September 11th has changed the world media landscape, where the main focus of media organisations has been on winning Arab hearts and minds. This has been clearly manifested in their new broadcasting strategies.

Chapter 1

Historical Development of the Arab Media

Overview of the development of the Arab media

Recent developments in the Arab media have taken the world by surprise. The monopoly of Al-Jazeera over the coverage of the war on Afghanistan is one of the main developments that Arab channels have witnessed most recently. The launch of Al-Jazeera English, Al-Hurra and Al-Arabiya is but one example of the rapid growth of Arab media. This growth came as a result of various political, social and economic changes that hit the Arab world. A brief historical review is useful to help understand and contextualise this development of the Arab media.

The media came into existence in Arab societies during the Western colonisation which goes back as far as 1797, when Napoleon invaded Egypt. The Turkish rule of Arab lands, and Christian missionaries have all contributed to the introduction of print media to Arab societies (Ayish 2001a). The chief objective of this media was both political and religious. Media outlets were employed to serve the colonisers' main agenda and propaganda. The prevailing oral culture in Arab societies made radio the most popular medium of communication. However, after the independence of most of these countries, both print media and radio adopted new local political and cultural strategies, which were geared towards encouraging development and nation-building. Print media and radio were under the control of Arab governments. Private media could not escape such control, which was justified by the desire of most Arab societies to break away from the message of colonisers, into a discourse of unity, social development and loyalty.

Ayish (2001a) divides the development of Arab media into three historical phases: the colonial phase, the post-colonial phase and the 1990s phase. The colonial phase was geared towards developing media technologies in order to promote the colonial propaganda message.

The post-colonial phase was, however, different in its focus and approach. It was characterised by 'the dominant paradigm' and attempts to shape media as a tool in order to serve national transformation and independence. The first stage witnessed a growth in literacy rates and the development of political institutionalisation (Ayish 2001a). The increase in literacy brought a growing demand for both Arab print and broadcast media. To meet this unprecedented demand, training centres and university courses were established to train journalists and media experts to take on this task (Ayish 2001a). This stage extended until the end of the 1980s.

The second stage of the post-colonial phase was characterised by the advent of new media technologies. These technologies contributed to the rapid distribution of media information in the Arab world, and in some cases managed to circumvent governments' control of media and information (Ayish 1991). This stage witnessed a revolution in the expansion of digital media. The political development in the region in the 1990s, such as the first Gulf War, gave this media the opportunity to test its technology. One of the key elements of this type of media is its transnational broadcast. We recall the monopoly of CNN over the flow of information and news related to the Gulf War: viewers across the globe tuned in to watch the war as it broke; national and state-controlled television had to rely on CNN in order to broadcast information.

The first Arabic printing press was set in Aleppo in Syria in 1706, and in Egypt by Mohamed Ali Pasha in 1819. Then the spread of print media reached Morocco (1820), Egypt (1828), Tunisia (1838), Syria (1865), Iraq (1869) and Libya (1866) (Abd al-Rahman 1996: 16–22). Egypt was the first Arab state to start radio service in the 1920s (Boyd 1993: 17), and was then followed by countries such as Tunisia, Morocco, Iraq, Jordan, Saudi Arabia, Lebanon, Algeria and Syria. Television came rather late to the Arab world, with the first channel launched in the mid-1950s. The arrival of television channels induced governments to invest in hiring expertise and developing means of communication. Universities across the Arab world started focusing on communication and media studies. This phase can be characterised as a governmental attempt to keep both media and expertise under its protective wings. However, the 1960s witnessed a rapid growth in media technologies. Arab audiences were no longer confined to the local media, but used transistor radio receivers to listen to international radio broadcasting from America and Europe (Ayish 1991). These international radios constituted a major source of information for the Arab public. The difference in both style and discourse made Arab listeners rely quite substantially on these broadcasters. But despite this, the Arab public remained loyal to the local media. The surfacing of audio and video cassette recorders in the 1970s made a big difference to the development of communication in the Arab world.

In the 1990s the media landscape of the Arab world changed dramatically. This phase ushered in a new digital era, which was clearly visible during the Gulf War, where CNN controlled the flow of information to the world in general and the Arab world in particular. This phase witnessed the proliferation of satellite channels globally, and this had an impact on the Arab world, which in turn started investing in the expansion and development of the Arab media. In addition to the existing satellite ARABSAT, which was established in 1976, in 2000 the Arab world witnessed the launch first of the Egyptian satellite system NILESAT and then, in 2000, the satellite THURAYYA, which contributed to providing information to both the private and government sectors. The mid-1990s saw a mushrooming of Arab satellite channels, which numbered sixty by the end of 1997. Private television services also experienced an increase. Some of the most active private channels were Middle Eastern Broadcasting Centre (MBC) in London, Orbit Television and Radio Network in Rome, Arab Radio and Television Network (ART), Future Television International (Lebanon), the Lebanese Broadcasting Corporation (LBC),

Al-Jazeera, Arab News Network (ANN) based in London and Al-Arabiya based in the UAE. These private media channels have contributed to the dissemination of news information beyond the geographical boundaries of their headquarters. The advent of these satellite channels has put Arab state television under enormous pressure. Arab governments have found it extremely difficult to control the flow of unfiltered information generated by these satellites.

The Arab media and Arab nationalism

Like the print media, after the independence of most of the Arab countries, the audio-visual media sought to preserve Arab unity and identity. Radio and television were seen as the appropriate channels of communication to reach out to the Arab public, some of whom were illiterate; however, these means of communication were state-owned or sponsored systems. Because of the popularity of radio and television among the Arab public, the information was filtered before being publicly aired. News bulletins were dominated by domestic activities and ceremonial occasions of state (Schleifer 2006).

Amin (2001) has categorised Arab radio and television into two groups. The first group exercised total control over radio and television. Both radio and television were and still are valued by the Arab public. Although television was introduced relatively late to the Arab world, with the first television being in Morocco in 1954, it was always regarded as the appropriate means of communication between governments and their citizens. In some Arab countries, however, radio and television were used transnationally to broadcast political messages and to mobilise the Arab public. After the Egyptian revolution in 1952, Gamal Abdel Nasser put much effort and energy into developing radio as a means of communication to reach out to the whole Arab world. Broadcasts were designed to mobilise the Arab public, and also to promote the Arab nationalists' ideas. Although his move was unpopular among some Arab governments such as Saudi Arabia, Nasser believed that the only way to bring down these governments was to mobilise their own people against them. On 4 July 1953, Cairo Radio broadcast its first programme, *Voice of the Arabs*. The programme aired anti-colonial messages (James 2006). Later on, Voice of the Arabs became a major station, broadcasting the Egyptian regime's ideology for eighteen hours each day across the Arab world (James 2006). Voice of the Arabs set out to achieve two main objectives, the first of which was to rise against imperialism, and the second to inform the Arab public of its 'own governments' sins' (James 2006). Voice of the Arabs successfully contributed to the overthrow of the Imam of Yemen in September 1962. Before that, in 1958, it mobilised the Arab nationalist group who staged a coup d'état to force Nuri to flee Baghdad, only to be captured and killed afterwards. The impact of Voice of the Arabs on the Arab street could not be ignored by most of the Arab regimes, notably King Saud of Saudi Arabia. He and his family were under close scrutiny and constant attack from the Voice of the Arabs in its programme *Enemies of God*. This led the Saudis to launch their own radio to counter-attack Nasser's Voice of the Arabs station.

Voice of the Arabs had drawn its aims and objectives from Voice of America (VOA) Arabic. Voice of America was launched to provide fair and transparent discussion on American policies and values. It was launched to air American propaganda during the Second World War, the Cold War and the Swiss crisis. Equally, Voice of the Arabs was launched to spread Nasser's propaganda to other Arab states, especially Saudi Arabia and Yemen. It was used as a platform to spread the idea of Arab nationalism and Arab unity. Voice of the Arabs was successful in mobilising and rallying the Arab public to support the idea that Arabs are one entity and one nation. Western critics, and indeed some Arab critics, consider Voice of the Arabs to be a colonising voice, with the intention of winning Arab hearts and minds, and subsequently mobilising them against their rulers, as well as foreign occupations.

Today, Radio Sawa and Al-Hurra face the same charges. Their mission of spreading freedom and democracy could not go unnoticed by some critics who have regarded this mission as an invasion of Arab hearts and minds. Both Sawa and Al-Hurra were launched to mobilise the Arab public to support the invasion of Iraq and American foreign policy in the Middle East. If Nasser's main objective of launching Voice of the Arabs was to mobilise the Arab public against its rulers, Sawa and Al-Hurra's mission was to mobilise the Arab public to support the US government's policies in the region. Despite being different in many ways, it could be said that Voice of the Arabs and Sawa have a few things in common. Both radio stations have called for, supported and encouraged the Arab public to be free. Voice of the Arabs called upon Yemenis and Saudis to rise against the hegemony of their governments and rulers. Equally, the US government's message through Al-Hurra and Sawa was that Iraqis deserved to be free from the rule of 'Saddam's tyranny and oppression'. This message fell on deaf ears and most Iraqis and Arabs took no notice of it. This is explained by the percentage of audiences that tune in to watch Al-Hurra or listen to Sawa.

Voice of the Arabs, however, was successful in encouraging the Arab public to embrace Nasser's ideas. The Egyptian media influence on the Arab world started with radio and then flourished through the exportation of the film industry. Egyptian movies have invaded Arab sitting rooms in the same way as Nasser's speeches invaded Arab minds. Nasser's attack on Saudi Arabia severed relations between the two countries, and sparked complaints from Crown Prince Faisal to the United States. The Crown Prince raised Nasser's attack on Saudi Arabia with both President Eisenhower and his successor, President Kennedy. The interference of Nasser in Yemen increased the Saudi government's concerns, and they no longer considered the Yemen unrest beyond their borders (Mejcher 2004). The civil war in Yemen between the royalists and republicans was cause for concern for Saudi Arabia. Such unrest in neighbouring Yemen induced Crown Prince Faisal to ask the US government to rein in Nasser who, in Faisal's eyes, represented communism. However, Kennedy at that time believed that any isolation of Nasser would pave the way for the Soviet Union to provide assistance and support to Nasser. The following passage gives us an insight into Kennedy's thoughts:

> While we are sympathetic to the position of Saudi Arabia, we are persuaded that both the Saudi Royal Family and other leaders might be more harmed than helped if the US should withdraw aid from the UAR [United Arab Republic] and leave the latter no alternative except to rely wholly on the Soviet Union. By our aid we hope gradually to divert Nasser's

attention from external probing and towards his great internal problems, primarily economic development. In the long run our goal is to establish a strong position in a key country and to entoil [*sic*] the UAR in the Western world through the advantages the UAR will gain therefrom.[1]

I have quoted at length Kennedy's policy in the Middle East during the Cold War to demonstrate the impact of the media on diplomacy in the region at that time. Despite Nasser's engagement in propaganda against other Arab regimes, Kennedy's administration resorted to the power of persuasion and dialogue with him; however, US diplomacy and communication with Nasser did nothing to lessen Faisal's main concerns, nor did they stop Nasser from broadcasting his anti-royal messages. The radio, which had long been envisaged as a means of communication, was now utilised as a means of promoting political agenda against regimes beyond the Egyptian borders. One could conclude that radio during Nasser's era was active in spreading Nasserism, Arab nationalism. It was also considered to be a potent weapon for mobilising the Arab public against its own governments. Nasser's media propaganda induced many Arab regimes to develop their own media to respond to the hostile messages he was broadcasting. This led to the proliferation of the Arab audio-visual media, and hence the emergence of Arab satellite stations.

The decline of the Ottoman Empire and its culture turned some Arab cities such as Beirut into cultural and political capitals, and the Arabic national discourse started to gather momentum. Some writers, thinkers and politicians formed networks to discuss Arab nationalism, identity and the Arab nation-state in the Middle East. The discussion was centred on how to bring Arabs, irrespective of their religious background, to serve the purpose of Arab unity. The Arab press played a significant part in the dissemination and development of these ideas. It was fully behind the original idea of one Arab nation based on one language and culture, and not religion. The notion of *al-qawmiyyah al-Arabia* (pan-Arabism) invaded every home in the Arab world. The idea of *qawmiyyah* was developed to counter the colonial powers targeting the Arab world. One of the fundamental pillars of *qawmiyyah* is the concept of one Arab state without borders.

Arab migrating media

During the 1970s some Arab media was under Arab government tight control. Its operation and broadcast were fully monitored. As a result, some of the Arab media choose foreign countries as a base for their operations. London and Paris were two of the most popular destinations for the Arab media. London, in particular, was regarded as the hub for migrating Arab media (Kraidy and Khalil 2009), being chosen for its strategic location and its liberal stance compared with other cities. Not only was London unrivalled as a communication centre, but it offered state-of-the-art technology and freedom of expression, and was well placed to distribute material across the Arab world and to the Arab diaspora in Europe. London was also chosen because it was traditionally known as a refuge for political oppositions and dissidents. These opposition groups used London as a base to promote their political ideas, agendas and mobilise the Arab public against its own rulers.

London was and still is the home for some well-established pan-Arab daily newspapers such as *Asharq Al-Awsat*; *Al-Arab*, a pro-Libyan newspaper; *Al-Quds Al-Arabi*, the Palestinian Arab nationalist voice; and *Al-Hayat*, a Lebanese newspaper. After realising the strategic location and importance of these media, some Arab governments have set up their own newspapers to promote their policies outside the geographical borders of their own states. Examples of this genre of newspaper are Egypt's *Al-Ahram* and the Iraqi ruling party's *Al-Thawra* (Jarrah 2008). Their principle audience is not expatriates, but foreign readers (Jarrah 2008). What sets these newspapers apart from the state media is their determination to cover stories without any censorship. Exile offers them the opportunity to operate without any control or constraints. The exile media have sought the exertion of political influence on the Arabic public, rather than commercial benefit (Jarrah 2008). Despite its pitfalls and shortcomings, the Arab media in exile has managed to foster a sense of debate, encourage dialogue and raise awareness of the status quo in the Arab world. It has also offered platforms for dissidents and oppositions to make their voices heard.

The number of newspapers which consider London as their base has, however, dwindled over the last few years. This is due to the ability of some Arab countries to offer the modern media technology and infrastructure needed by most media organisations. This, coupled with the high cost of living and tax charges for operating from London, has driven some media outlets out of London.

The Gulf crisis has made London again a launch-pad for satellite news broadcasting. MBC and BBC Arabic television, both Saudi-sponsored channels, managed to make an impact on their Arab viewers; however, this impact did not last long after the channels were taken off air because of disagreements over editorial independence. The BBC aired an episode of *Panorama* on 4 April 1996 which was very critical of Saudi Arabia's record on human right issues. The Saudi government accused the BBC of failing to consider Saudi sensitivities. This led to the termination of the BBC Arabic contract (Kraidy and Khalil 2009). The collapse of MBC Arabic has given way to the rise of Al-Jazeera Arabic, which has benefited tremendously from the expertise and professionalism of MBC staff.

Print media

The Arab world has some very common features that distinguish it from other countries. Arab countries share the same language, culture and almost the same religion; however, print media varies quite extensively from one state to another (Amin 2001). Its development has been very slow, which can be explained by the high rate of illiteracy in the Arab world. Print media seems to develop and gather momentum in countries where the level of literacy is quite high, such as Lebanon; however, where the level of literacy is low, the development and circulation of print media is quite limited.

As the statistics in Table 1.1 show, the rate of illiteracy is still quite high in most Arab countries. This explains why audio-visual media is still popular among the Arab public. Although these people enjoy tuning in to watch television programmes, for instance, they lack the skills and ability to critically engage with the information they consume. This category of people (although not in all cases) could be described as the passive recipients of information.

Table 1.1 *Illiteracy in the Arab world. (Source: http://middleeast.about. com/od/middleeast101/a/me090425b.htm; statistics compiled from United Nations, 2009 World Almanac,* The Economist)

Rank	Country	Illiteracy rate (%)
1	Mauritania	49
2	Morocco	48
3	Yemen	46
4	Sudan	39
5	Djibouti	32
6	Algeria	30
7	Iraq	26
8	Tunisia	25.7
9	Egypt	28
10	Syria	19
11	Oman	18
12	Saudi Arabia	17.1
13	Libya	16
14	Bahrain	13
15	Lebanon	12
16	UAE	11.3
17	Qatar	11
18	Jordan	9
19	Palestine	8
20	Kuwait	7

Other major factors that have contributed to the underdevelopment of print media in the Arab world are censorship, rigid press laws and regulations, and limited means of circulation and dissemination of materials (Amin 2001).

The development of the Arab media varies from one Arab country to another. A review of the history of print media in the Arab world takes us back to 1816, with *Journal Al-Iraq* as the first Arab newspaper. The first daily newspaper started in 1873. One of the main characteristics of the early newspapers is the fact that they were considered as the voice of the ruling parties. They promoted the official political line, agendas and ideas. This meant that the press in general was designed to serve the ruling parties, rather than the Arab public, and this was a common feature across the Arab world. The newspapers played a significant role in promoting governments' domestic achievements to Arab citizens and the world (Amin 2001). In a way, the Arab press was utilised as a propaganda tool to cement the official line. As such, most of the Arab press fell short in painting independently and impartially the true picture of Arab governments. It refrained from criticising the governments because it risked jeopardising the financial support it received from them; most of the Arab press relied in its early stages on government support (Azet 1992).

A comparative examination of Middle Eastern media and North African media indicates that the press in North Africa enjoyed a relaxation in press laws. In Algeria, for instance, a 'less restrictive information code was introduced' (Amin 2001: 25). In Tunisia, most of the newspapers were published in French, although Arabic is the official language and the mother tongue of the majority of Tunisians. In an attempt to relax press laws, the Tunisian government reviewed its press code and issued a new revised version in 1980, but there are many restrictions on the operation of the press in Tunisia.

The Moroccan approach is slightly different. Morocco is one of the Arab countries that have a well-developed press. A variety of newspapers are published in both Arabic and French, representing different parties and governmental sectors. The opposition press are granted the opportunity to criticise the government and its performance, although no criticism of the monarchy is tolerated. Since King Mohamed VI ascended to the throne, the press in Morocco has grown in both number and confidence. Some of the newspapers have adopted a more liberal approach and started operating freely and without restrictions.

The first newspaper to emerge in Morocco was a Spanish paper entitled *Africa Liberal*, published in 1820. This was followed by the first Arabic newspaper, *Al Maghrib*, in 1886 (Azzi 1998). According to Tafasca (1984), Morocco witnessed a proliferation of newspapers between 1820 and 1912, with over fifty titles published in French and Spanish by European settlers. One of the aims of these newspapers was to advance the colonial agenda and promote both the French and Spanish languages.

Away from the traditional Moroccan press, the contemporary Moroccan press can be traced back to World War II. The Moroccan nationalist party, Istiqlal Party, launched its Arabic newspaper, *Al-'Alam* in Arabic, and *L'Opinion* in French, both of which were geared towards promoting independence and resisting colonial powers, especially the French occupation. Both papers gained Moroccan public trust and were able to mobilise the Moroccan public to rise against occupation and colonialism. The name of the nationalist party was also very revealing. The name 'Istiqlal' in Arabic means 'independence', and this has attracted quite a high percentage of Moroccans who resisted the occupation. Besides these two papers, there were two main dailies: *La Vigie* and *Le Petit Marocain*, both of which were published by the French-owned company, Mas group. Although Rugh (1979) considered these two newspapers to be non-politically oriented, Tafasca (1984) provided a different account of their functionalities, one of which was to serve the French administration in Morocco. Since Moroccan independence, different parties have owned the country's newspapers, which often serve as the voice of the party. The Moroccan press has generally enjoyed relative freedom of expression. The 1958 press legislation demonstrated 'the desire of different political parties to preserve this space of free expression' (Azzi 1998: 5). This desire is still prevalent among most of the Moroccan parties. The audio-visual media has also enjoyed relative freedom.

The development of the Moroccan media has gathered momentum over the last two decades or so. Today, there is a proliferation of dailies reflecting the Moroccan political landscape. As one shops around, one cannot help noticing the wide range of newspapers that reflect different political parties: liberal, conservative and left-wing newspapers, in addition to private and independent ones. What makes some of these dailies, such as *Al Muharrir* and *Al Bayan*, more interesting is their opposition to the government; in a way, they serve as the opposition voice. According to Ibahrine (2002), the media in Morocco has changed since the late 1990s, becoming 'rigorous, active and pluralistic'. This is attributed to the relaxation of regulatory restriction and the growth in newspaper publication (Hegasy 1997). This relaxation came as a result of the removal of the interior minister in 1999, which not only opened the gate for the inception of new newspapers, but also gave the existing ones the opportunity to touch upon previously taboo issues such as human rights.

The press in Algeria was predominantly French oriented and was used to serve the French administration in Algeria. In addition to the French press, there were some locally distributed newspapers published in Arabic.

Al Haq was the first Muslim paper to be published, in 1983 in the city of Annaba. The paper was committed to highlighting the suffering of Muslims and the 'oppressive policies to expropriate the lands of Muslims' (Azzi 1998: 5). Because of its open criticism of occupation, the paper was banned; however, this gave rise to other Algerian newspapers that adopted the same stance. *El Farrouq, Al Siddiq* and *Thu El Fekar* were other newspapers that took the same line of argument as *Al Haq*. They were mainly focused on highlighting the plight of the Algerian people under their French colonial masters.

The 1920s witnessed a change in Algerian society in terms of leadership and voices calling for independence. Among these voices was Sheikh Ibn Badis, who was educated in Al-Azhar. Upon his return, Ibn Badis launched a reform campaign that would transform Algerian society. The reform was intended to put Algeria's house in order before any attempt was made to take on the colonial power. Ibn Badis addressed issues such as rituals and myths that were practised and believed to contradict the teaching of Islam. Ibn Badis also called for the revival of Islamic culture and the protection of Islamic identity 'in the face of colonial attempts to eliminate this dimension and assimilate the Muslims into the colonial culture' (Azzi 1998: 5–6). The first attempt of Ibn Badis and his followers was to establish religious schools which would help in the revival of Islamic culture and renaissance, following in the footsteps of Muslim reformists such as Mohammad Abdu and Jamal Eddine Al Afghani. Ibn Badis and his followers recognised the importance of the press and used it effectively. Ibn Badis's first newspaper, *al-Montaqid*, did not last long and was banned in the year of its inception (Azzi 1998: 6); however, this did not deter Ibn Badis from continuing to raise awareness of the importance of Islamic culture and identity.

The first Algerian Muslim Ulama Association chose the journal

El Bacair to represent its views. The association's main impetus was to safeguard and preserve Islamic identity. The journal lasted longer than was expected.

A review of the Algerian press's historical development indicates that it experienced rapid growth after World War II because of the popularity of Muslim nationalist press. Most of the Muslim nationalist press were weeklies, such as *La République Algérienne*, *El Bacair* and *El Moujahid*, among others. These weeklies were banned in the first year of the war for independence. After independence, there was a proliferation of newspapers representing different political thought; however, this state of affairs ceased to exist when the parliament announced that Algeria was a one-party state. Most of the newspapers were nationalised, including *La Dépêche d'Alger*, *L'Echo d'Oran* and *La Dépêche de Constantine*, which had a tremendous effect on the multiplicity and diversity of the press. Today, however, Algeria has a wide range of dailies and weeklies, such as *Ech-chaab*, *El-Khabar*, *El-Massa*, *Essabah*, *Ennahar El-Djadid*, *Echourouk El Youmi*, *Le Quotidien d'Algérie* and *La Nouvelle République*. Some of these newspapers are written in Arabic and French, but the most striking point is that most of these newspapers' titles connote change and a new era (new day, the morning, etc.).

Unlike the Moroccan and Algerian press, the Tunisian press was allowed to develop during the time of French colonialism. Most of the newspapers were in French and were designed to target the middle class. The nationalist press, however, unlike in Algeria and Morocco, was not allowed to flourish. For instance, *L'Action Tunisienne* was closely monitored and controlled by the French administration, only to be closed down in 1933 (Azzi 1998: 9).

After independence, the Tunisian press was very supportive of the government. They helped in promoting the government's policies and political activities without any criticism. It should be said that the Tunisian press lacked diversity and multiplicity, due to the lack of a multi-party system. The mid-1980s witnessed a new, more relaxed government approach in dealing with the press, as a result of which few new newspapers emerged to the surface. There was also an extensive foreign press presence in Tunisia from both European and Arab countries.

Today, Tunisia has a number of dailies and weeklies, but they are fewer in number than in other Arab countries. Among the popular weeklies and dailies are *Al-Sabah, Alhorria, L'Economiste Maghrébin, Le Quotidien, Réalités* and *Le Temps*. As their titles suggest, these newspapers and magazines are written in either Arabic or French.

Egypt can be said to have one of the most developed press in the Arab world, with Cairo considered the hub for the major publications. In the past, the Egyptian press was very cautious in criticising and libelling the government; however, in 1996 a new code was introduced and journalists and reporters have been given relative freedom to express their views without fear of being imprisoned or reprimanded (Amin 2001). The most influential newspapers in Egypt are *Al-Ahram, Al-Akhbar* and *Al-Jumhuriyah*. Today, Egypt offers a wide range of newspapers in Arabic and English, representing different groups, parties and voices.

The press in Libya is state-run and reflects the official government line. The most popular newspaper in Libya is *Wakalat Al-Anba' Al-Jamahiriya* (Jamahiriya News Agency [JANA]). It has a monopoly on news distribution and so is the only single source of domestic news (Amin 2001) and, according to Amin (2001: 26), JANA 'is the sole authorized distributor of foreign news'. The Libyan press remains the most underdeveloped in North Africa.

The political unrest that swept Sudan over the last two decades has meant that the media are under the tight control of the government. The army holds control of most of the newspapers. Mindful of external criticism, the government launched an English-language weekly, *New Horizon*, where they try to explain the official line. Sudan has a range of Arabic dailies and weeklies, such as *Al-Ayaam, Al-Sahafa, Al-Intibaha, Hilal al Sudan, Alakhbar, Al-Wifaq* and *Alahdath*.

The Syrian press has always maintained the structure and form of the communist states. Most of the newspapers were in the hands of the communist party and there is little or no freedom of expression (Amin 2001). The press is designed to mobilise the Syrian public to support the Baa'tist, the country's ruling party. The same can be said of the press in neighbouring Iraq during the 1980s and 1990s, where the press had no freedom of expression and was mobilised in support of the Iraqi government, mainly the Baa'tist. The Iran–Iraq war had rallied the press in Iraq to support the official line, and support the ruling party, as any attempt to deviate from the official line would have meant the newspaper in question was taking the Iranians' side. In addition to being loyal to the state, journalists were often aware of the grave consequences they would face if they reported against the state or the government on any matter. The Iraqis' access to satellite television came in 1999 after the ministry of information published a plan to keep the dissemination of information under state control. Before the invasion, there were five main newspapers accessed by Iraqis. In 2003, Paul Bremer, the interim governor in Iraq, abolished the ministry of information. This led to the proliferation of privately owned media and by 2006, there were about sixty Iraqi channels, representing diverse political and religious views (Kraidy and Khalil 2009). There were sub-national channels as well as national ones. Al-Hurra-Iraq is a national channel funded by US Congress. Later on, Iraq launched the Al-Iraqiya channel as part of the Iraqi Media Network (IMN). Al-Iraqiya has become a viable weapon in the hands of the ruling parties, while sub-national channels remain privately owned and work to serve the political and ideological interest of their owners. The mushrooming of the media in Iraq 'reflects different established and emerging voices in Iraq' (Kraidy and Khalil 2009: 30). Examples of these channels are *Al-Zawra'*, *Alsumaria*, *Al-Fayha'* and *Al-Sharqiya*. The ownership of these channels by Iraqi factions could have some knock-on effects on the dissemination of news and information of national interest. Small newspapers will be interested in serving the interests of their groups, and this might have some repercussions on national unity.

Unlike Syria and Iraq, Jordan's press laws are relaxed and private media is allowed to operate freely, though not entirely. The desire to boost the economy and develop the country's infrastructure has pushed the Jordanian government to encourage private investment, and media is one of the sectors involved. The Jordanian press is partly state-owned and partly privately owned (Amin 2001). All press in Jordan must acquire a licence from the government in order to be able to publish. *Al-Ray* remains the most influential state-owned newspaper. Other newspapers include *Addustour*, *Al-Arab Al-Yawm*, *Al Ghad* and *Jordan Times*.

The Yemeni press can be divided into two: a press in support of the liberal South, and a press in support of the conservative North. The marriage of the North and South has meant that the press now represents the whole of Yemeni state. Before the marriage, the press in the South was under the tight control of the government, while the press in the North enjoyed relative freedom of expression. The press developed quite rapidly after the merger of South and North, however, and different newspapers now represent different parties. Among the Arabic newspapers in Yemen are *Al Ahale*, *Al-Mo'tamar*, *Al Thawra*, *Al-Ayyam*, *Al Sahwa* and *Al Wahda*. Apart from the latter, they are dailies. In addition to Arabic newspapers, Yemen has a relatively limited number of English newspapers such us *Yemen Observer*, *Yemen Post* and *Yemen Times*. Other Arabic newspapers, such as *Al-Mo'tamar*, provide an English translation.

Compared with other Arab states, Lebanon's press enjoys more freedom in its coverage. Because Lebanon has the highest level of literacy, the consumption of news is higher. Despite the civil war that ravaged the country, there is a wide range of newspapers published in both Arabic and English. The Lebanese press remains the most developed press in the region. It consists of a wide range of newspapers produced in Arabic, French and English. Some of the press represent political parties; others represent the government. But the most interesting issue here is the diversity and variety of the press. Some newspapers are very liberal while others do still maintain a level of conservatism. The Arabic Lebanese newspapers include *Al Akhbar*, *Al-Anbaa*, *Al Balad*, *Al Binaa*, *Al Hawadeth*, *Al Hayat* and *Al Intiqad*. English newspapers include *Al-Nabad*, *Lebanon News* and *Monday Morning*; newspapers in French include *L'Hebdo Magazine* and *L'Orient-Le Jour*.

By tradition the press of the Gulf States is conservative. It is state-owned and designed to support and promote the official line (Amin 2001). Most of the newspapers are published in Arabic, but publications in English have recently become available. The press code of practice is strictly controlled by the government, especially in Saudi Arabia.

Saudi Arabia is the largest state in the Gulf and one that has tight control of the media. A committee consisting of representatives from different government ministries has been established to monitor 'local and foreign publications' (Amin 2001: 27). The kingdom has a wide range of daily newspapers that cover all sorts of themes, some of which are published outside the country. The most established English newspaper is the *Saudi Gazette*.

Unlike Saudi Arabia, Kuwait has a diverse press, some privately owned, and others state-owned, representing different voices and views. Kuwait has a relaxed press code and newspapers enjoy relative freedom of publication. Dar Al-Siyassa, Dar Al-Rai Al-'am and Dar Al Qabas are the leading publishing houses in Kuwait (Amin 2001). There are many newspapers written in Arabic and English, including *Al Watan, Alam Al Yawm, Annahar, Arab Times, Desert Voice, Economic Weekly* and *Kuwait Times*.

Qatar's press has developed rapidly over the last few years, with *Wakalat Al-Anba Al-Qatariya* (Qatar News Agency) being the main source of news in the country. Other dailies are *Al-Raya, Al-Arab* and *Al-Sharq*. The leading English newspaper is the *Gulf Times*.

The press in the United Arab Emirates is diverse and has a variety of Arabic and English newspapers. *Al Ittihad* newspaper was established in 1972 and still remains the leading Arabic newspaper in the UAE. The *Emirates News* is the main English newspaper published in the UAE; however, because of the economic development that has taken place in the UAE and the excessive immigration, especially of English-speaking immigrants, a number of English newspapers have been established to cater for the high demand for English publications by Western expatriates.

The press in Palestine was slow to progress in its early stages partly because of political orientations among the Palestinian parties, and partly because of the occupation. Today, despite economic sanctions, Palestine enjoys a wide range of daily newspapers, which represent all factions in the West Bank and Gaza. Some of these newspapers are liberal and others are conservative, reflecting the voices of the parties or groups they represent.

Radio and television

Arab radio and television emerged after the independence of most of the Arab countries. Because of the Arab oral culture, radio and television are popular means of communication for the public. Governments have seized the opportunity to impose total state control over radio and television coverage. At first, the broadcasting institutions were mostly owned and controlled by the state (Amin 2001); however, over the last decade or so, Arab governments have opened up to the idea of diverse media outlets that can be owned by private institutions. These new media have created a new broadcasting culture where sensitive and taboo issues are discussed and debated within the state code of media practice.

Despite this mushrooming of radio and television in the Arab world, Arab governments maintained a desire to centralise the media in order to preserve national unity and culture. Radio and television are powerful weapons in the hand of the Arab government because they use them as a channel through which to publicise their political ideas. Controlling radio and television meant stifling the opposition who lacked these means of communication, especially since the majority of the Arab public are illiterate and do not have access to other means of communication (Boyd and Amin 1993). It should be noted here that most of the radio and television channels are subsided by the Arab governments, who ensure that these media outlets are in line with the government political line; however, the recent development of transnational radios and televisions has made the task of controlling and disseminating information difficult.

Amin (2001) divided Arab radio and television into two groups. The first group is designed to mobilise the public to support government policies and political ideas. This type of broadcasting operates in Algeria, Egypt, Iraq, Syria, Libya, Yemen and Sudan. These countries have used radio and television as a means of encouraging the public to rally behind the governments' policies and political ideas. The second group has tight control of radio and television, with the exception of Morocco and Lebanon (Amin 2001) which have adopted a more relaxed system of broadcasting where the media has relative freedom in covering issues related to the state and government. In most Arab states, radio started on a commercial basis relatively late. It was launched in Algeria in 1925, Egypt in 1926 and Tunisia in 1935. The radio stations' revenue is commercial.

Broadcasting in Morocco began during French rule, when radio was established during the 1920s and television appeared in 1954. The main aim of the launch of both radio and television was to serve the French communities in Morocco and Algeria. Most of the radio stations continued to broadcast after Moroccan independence; however, after 1959, the government took the decision to nationalise these networks and, where possible, to close down the commercial stations. This has paved the way for the creation of a national network, which later fell under government control. Midi 1 radio managed to break the silence, however, and adopt an aggressive broadcasting style based on impartial views. A huge number of audiences throughout North Africa would tune in to listen to very interesting news and information. Most of the programmes were aimed at entertaining the audience, rather than raising awareness of the political issues in Morocco.

Television came rather late, appearing in 1954, and not all Moroccans had access to television because the majority could not afford to purchase a television set. In the rural areas, radio was more popular than television.

Today, both radio and television are popular means of accessing information in Morocco. In addition to the government owned channel, al-Maghribiya, there are other private and transnational channels, among which are 2M, Al-Jazeera and other Arabic satellite channels. There is also a proliferation of medium- and short-wave radio stations, as well as transnational radio stations.

In addition to radio and television, the internet has become a major source of news and information, especially among the middle class. Although some people cannot afford a computer and the cost of subscribing to an internet network, they still use cyberspace. The young generation use the internet for educational purposes as well as for social networking.

Algeria witnessed its first radio broadcast in 1926, which was in French and was aimed at French settlers in Algiers (Azzi 1998: 10). Two radio stations began broadcasting in Arabic and Berber in 1947. In 1962, radio and television merged to form a national network called Radio-Télévision Algérienne (RTA). It should be mentioned here that both radio and television are government owned, so the dissemination of information is strictly controlled by the government. Unlike Morocco for instance, Algerian radio and television have yet to break some taboos such as criticising the government or offering a platform for opposition parties.

Azzi (1998: 13) distinguished between two media systems used in the Grand Maghrib. There is a government-sanctioned press system in Morocco and Tunisia, while there is an unstable state-controlled press system in Algeria. The first system controls information but allows for private ownership of newspapers; the second system strictly controls the operation of the media.

Some Arab governments have handed the task of establishing and administrating radios to foreign companies. Egypt, for instance, 'authorized the British Marconi Company' to run the government system from 1934 to 1948 (Amin 2001: 30). Similarly, Tunisia authorised a French company to establish radio broadcasting in 1939.

After 1945, both the press and radio in the Arab world were used as a weapon to fight colonialism and call for national independence. This phase witnessed a direct confrontation between the colonial powers and journalists who were advancing the cause of liberation and independence. This confrontation ended in 'brutal treatment' of journalists at the hands of colonial authorities, including 'torture, prison and exile' (Essoulami 2006).

Main hindrances to the development of the Arab media

While the media across the world has witnessed some substantial development both in numbers and delivery method, the development of the Arab media was very slow and at times static. This is attributed to a range of factors. According to Amin (2002: 125), the Arab media was slow to develop because of the 'weak economic base, close ties to politics and political movements'. It is no surprise that the slow growth of the economy in the Arab world has had an impact on the development of the media. The lack of investment in the communication sector in some parts of the Arab world meant some media had to rely on traditional means of communication, which made it extremely difficult for them to compete with other, well-equipped regional and international media. The association of media with political parties and most often its backing of the governments meant that the media lost the public's trust. The thriving notion of Arab nationalism had led some Arab media to promote this new phenomenon, which was very popular among Arab audiences. These factors, among others, have contributed to the slow development of Arab media, and the lack of diversity in Arab media outlets expresses the stagnation in the development of Arab media in general.

The loyalty of some journalists to certain political parties renders some reports incredible; however, the flow of information from transnational media meant that some Arab journalists started to think about freedom of expression and the right of the Arab public to be introduced to impartial and accurate information. This put them in an awkward position, especially those working for state-run media. They found themselves for the first time obliged to take a clear stance, either to support freedom of expression or support the governments' policies (Amin 1995).

This brings us to the censorship of Arab media. As mentioned earlier, the Arab public is more inclined towards audio-visual media than to print because of the high percentage of illiteracy in the Arab world. Knowing this, the Arab governments have maintained a tight grip on the dissemination of information. To quote Amin (2002: 126), 'electronic media are absolute monopolies under direct government supervision'. This includes filtering any information that is deemed controversial and which might affect the government's position. The media is used as a tool to promote cultural, political and government policies. Governed by the notion of respect and obedience, the Arab media tended to passively disseminate these policies without questioning their accuracy or authenticity. Over the last few years, however, and with the launch of new media outlets, some of the Arab media have moved away from the notion of obedience into adopting new principles of accountability and responsibility. These principles have strengthened the journalists' resolve to broadcast open and transparent information. Al-Jazeera and Al-Arabiya are two examples in point. As will be discussed in Chapter 3, these new channels have set new standards, which are based on freedom of expression and freedom of speech. Their colourful programmes have contributed quite extensively to offering open and free debate.

Transnational media

Transnational media in the Middle East start to evolve in the 1980s. The introduction of direct broadcast satellites (DBS) meant that broadcasters could reach the Arab audience without any control of information by the government. With the expansion of transnational media, the state-owned media found itself losing ground to these channels. The first Palestinian intifada was an example of how the state-owned television could not compete with Al-Jazeera, for instance, which was broadcasting live from the Palestinian territories. Millions of Arab viewers would watch the same broadcast, and this has created a unified strong Arab public opinion, manifested in the repeated demonstrations in the streets (Amin 2004). Without the transnational media, these types of demonstration would not have taken place.

Transnational Arab broadcasters have created platforms for debating the most controversial issues, and this has created a generation fully aware of their rights and obligations. As a result of the discussion of issues of utmost importance to the Arab world, the Arab public is no longer a passive audience who will accept information without questioning its authenticity. Examples of the mobilisation of the Arab public are clearly evident in the action taken by the Arab public sphere in its reaction to the Israeli invasion of both Lebanon and Gaza. Millions of people took to the streets to voice their opposition to the Israeli 'aggression' in a move to express their solidarity with the Palestinians. Amin (2004: 4) noted that:

> transnational broadcast news coverage about the Middle East conflict has a tremendous appeal to Arab audiences, since unlike print, it favours movement over stillness, simplification over complexity, specificity over abstraction and the present over the past or the future.

The new technology and methods of broadcasting utilised by transnational media have had a great impact on the Arab public. The combination of photography and comments in the coverage of events has had a tremendous effect on the way the Arab public approaches television. The coverage of the Arab–Israeli conflict and the recent wars in Iraq, Lebanon and Gaza changed the Arab media landscape. The Arab public was no longer restricted to the information provided by state-run television: satellite channels such as Al-Jazeera were broadcasting live and around the clock.

Transnational Arab media has created an open space for discussion, debate and understanding of the main national and international issues. Transnational media could be considered the opposition party in the Middle East. Through its broadcasting, it raises awareness of the political, economic and cultural issues in the region, and it contributes to the explanation of complex conflicts nationally and internationally. For Amin (2004: 8):

> Transnational broadcasting is providing the region with an unprecedented opportunity to share the thoughts and worries of the people in the region without fear. Transnational media are providing the world with a tremendous chance for developing the foundation of peace, an unprecedented forum for the exchange of views. Arab television stations are having secularists debating Islamists, Iraqis debating Kuwaitis and Israelis debating Palestinians.

In his discussion of the role of transnational media in forming public opinion, Amin (2004) notes that transnational media is the effective means through which we can change and have immense impact on global public opinion. An example of this is the impact Al-Jazeera has made in forming Arab public opinion, managing to deeply penetrate Arab communities. It has also contributed to expanding public access, strengthening regional understanding, and mobilising the Arab public to a shared purpose. In this context, it can be noted that there has been a change in both the way in which information is disseminated and the way in which the Arab public consumes and engages with this information. Arab state-run televisions now face stiff competition from transnational Arab media channels.

Cultural implications of transnational Arab television

Apart from providing a platform for opposition to air their voices, one of the main implications of transnational media in the Arab world is its role in strengthening the language and cultural ties between the Arab countries (Kraidy 2002). Individual Arab countries' festivals and cultural activities are often shared with the rest of the Arab world. For instance, we saw how the 2009 Asila festival in Morocco was covered on Al-Jazeera, and as a result, most Arab viewers have become aware of the cultural activities in Morocco. To borrow Kraidy's words, 'satellite television has brought about a pan-Arab consciousness' (2002: 7). Transnational Arab television has brought to Arab living rooms debates and discussion about topics that are of common interest to a larger Arab public, and no longer confined to individual Arab countries. The channels have also contributed to disseminating Arab music and other cultural activities. The wide range of programmes on offer by most of the transnational television channels is designed to engage the Arab public in debate and discussion. Al-Jazeera's *Crossfire* programme attracts viewers from across the Arab world, some of whom call in to express their views, while others complete entries on the channel's website. Programmes such as this have contributed to raising awareness of Arab issues among the Arab public.

There are some in the Arab world who oppose transnational television, however, because they feel it disseminates material which could be considered a threat to Arab culture. Some consider these channels a means of promoting Western culture and values (Kraidy 2002: 8). They are particularly concerned about the impact these channels have on traditional family values, and some have laid the blame on transnational media for the erosion of family values in the Arab world. This is because, they claim, the new generation is influenced by transnational media which promotes individualism over the long-established tradition of family unity.

In his report *A Strategy to Improve a Negative American Image in the Middle East* (2005), Lieutenant Colonel Dickinson asserted that Arab opinions about the United States are formed through the influence of the Arab media. He pointed to the broadcast of images of violence in the West Bank and Gaza Strip, which are aired through audio-visual media to millions of Arabs and Muslims across the globe. This has often generated debate about the role of the US in the Palestinian–Israeli conflict. Dickinson recognised the importance of the Arab media and its impact on the Arab public sphere, stating 'Satellite television, newspapers, magazines and radios have the greatest impact in the region because they reach the largest audience' (2005: 7). Indeed, as mentioned earlier, the Arab public tends to incline towards audio-visual media, but recently, with the increasing rate of literacy, they have started to have access to print media. The impact of the Arab media, according to Dickinson, is evident in the Arab public's negative perception of the United Sates. The Arab public, he goes on to say, tends to believe what has been covered by the media, although this is not a true reflection of reality. Dickinson's remarks are significant because first, they demonstrate quite clearly how powerful the Arab media is in mobilising the Arab public to take action; and second, they show that the reliance of the Arab public on the media has grown quite rapidly.

Historical development of satellite television in the Arab world

Since the late 1960s, the Arab media has witnessed both political and technical development (Kraidy 2002). The main goal of the Arab satellite television channels, as articulated by Arab ministers, is 'the integration of the social and cultural activities of the Arab league' (Kraidy 2002: 2). The Arab States Broadcasting Union (ASBU) was established in 1969. Saudi Arabia did not join the Union, but joined the 1976 Arab Satellite Communications orga-nisation (ARABSAT), which was established to promote the cultural and educational needs of the Arab world. Saudi Arabia was the main financier of the organisation, which took Riyadh as its headquarters.

Other Arab governments established their own channels in subsequent years. The mid-1990s witnessed an expansion in media satellite channels, including the launch of Al-Jazeera and ANN. The rapid expansion of the Arab media can be traced back to the Cold War and the Gulf War. The dominance of CNN's unfiltered coverage of the Gulf War made Arab governments realise for the first time the tangible threat of transnational satellite television and alerted them to the importance of transnational media. According to Khatib, a senior employee of Al-Arabiya channel, the Arab public 'realised that all the information they were getting from Arab sources – whether government or from Iraqis or from Kuwaitis or from their own media about the war – was fake'.[2] Indeed, most of the Arab public, especially the elite who had access to the international transnational media, found a big disparity between the coverage of the state-owned channels and the coverage of transnational media such as CNN. This generated many questions about the objectivity and accuracy of information imparted by the state-owned media.

The success of CNN's broadcasting and hegemony over the dissemination of news induced some Arab governments and media organisations to launch new satellites (Vogt 2002). This led to the creation of the Middle East Broadcasting Center (MBC) in 1991, which was geared towards marrying entertainment and education. The inclusion of an entertainment aspect came about because of fierce competition from some private media companies. Also launched in response to CNN's dominance were Arab Radio and Television (ART), ORBIT and the Egyptian Satellite Channel (ESC). Contrary to the state-owned media, most of the new Arab channels think that the best way to gain credibility and popularity among the Arab public is through providing an objective and impartial coverage of the news.

State media and satellite channels

The advent of satellite channels in the region has placed the state-run television channels in an awkward position. The flow of information, irrespective of national geographical borders, has made it quite difficult for Arab governments to control this information. Some of the interactive programmes on these channels have encouraged free and open debate; a new approach which has taken both Arab governments and the Arab public by surprise. In a departure from the traditional approach, often adopted by state-run television, of inviting a guest to answer a series of questions put to him/her by a journalist, the Arab public has been introduced to a new style and platform for debating issues, no matter how controversial they may be. At times, these debates touch upon sensitive issues such as political leaders, style of governance and women's issues. According to Kraidy (2002: 5) 'Satellite television talk-shows serve as a catalyst for a democratic renewal, where Arab audience members would mobilise as citizens and become increasingly interested in participation in democratic politics.'

In an unprecedented move, some Arab governments have allowed a level of freedom to the satellite channels, although some of the channels do still exercise caution in their coverage of sensitive issues. Arab government channels, however, are often used as powerful means to criticise and attack other Arab leaders.

History of the freedom of the press in the Arab world

The freedom of the press in the Arab world can only be understood when it is placed within its wider social, cultural and political context. The independence of most of the Arab countries was characterised by the abolition of the multi-party system (Amin 2002), and this had a knock-on effect on the operation of the media in general. Most of the countries in the region were subject to a one-party rule, which limited freedom of expression from the mid-1950s until the mid-1980s. If we take, for instance, Egypt, Nasser realised from the early days of his governance that controlling the media was the best way to control people's minds. Not only did he succeed in doing that, but he managed to mobilise people against their own governments.

In some Arab countries, journalists are often subjected to intimidation and questioning, either by opposition groups or state agents. In Algeria, for instance, the eruption of the post-1992 elections violence widened the divide between the government and the Islamists. As a consequence, journalists supporting both sides were targeted. According to Mantzikos (2007: 14), 'the clampdown on news coverage gradually extended to independent Arabic publications which had been critical of the government.' It is worth mentioning here that the Algerian constitution guarantees the freedom of the press. But that was dealt a severe knock when in 2006 the government 'passed a decree that granted immunity to perpetrators of violence during the conflict (the Algerian civil war)' (Mantzikos 2007: 14). The decree was seen by some as a decisive blow to those journalists who had disappeared or were subjected to violent acts. The decree also authorised imprisonment of up to five years for anyone who 'exploited the wounds of the National Tragedy' (Mantzikos 2007: 14). The first victim of this decree was the journalist Bachir Larabi, who was sentenced to a month in jail for defaming a local mayor.

While countries such as Algeria continue to pass decrees to protect their national unity, other countries such as Morocco and Mauritania have adopted more relaxed rules which ensure freedom of expression in both countries. Mauritania, for instance, established in 2005 the National Commission in Charge of the Reform of the Press and Broadcasting. In addition, in 2006, the government created the High Authority for the Press and Broadcasting (HAPA), an independent regulatory body (Mantzikos 2007: 14). Although the government still maintains control over the television and radio, their move of establishing an independent regulatory body could be considered a step in the right direction, a step which I think could create a culture of freedom of expression in this small North African country. As a result of this regulatory body, many privately owned newspapers were launched in Mauritania.

To understand the major changes that have affected the course of the freedom of the press in the Middle East, one ought to take a step back and review the historical context of the Arab media. Newspapers have existed in the region since the eighteenth century, and initially were under the strict control of the Ottoman authorities or foreign powers. Recent global technological developments, however, have enabled the Arab media to expand beyond recognition. International 'events like the decolonization, the end of the USA–USSR cold war conflict, the 11/9 [*sic*] terrorist attacks and the US response, have influenced not only the regimes but also the populations of the Arab countries' (Tassopoulos 2007: 8). The development of the media meant that Arab governments were less in control of the circulation of news and information. Gaining its freedom of broadcasting, the Arab media started flirting with oppositions who were often very critical of their governments and regimes. Nonetheless, some Arab governments have done all they could to keep a tight control of the media.

Although the openness of the Arab media is for the good of the Arab public, some Islamic groups, such as al-Qaeda, have taken full advantage of these relaxed rules and managed to broadcast their messages to the Arab and Muslim public. The wide dissemination of al-Qaeda's messages is but one tangible example of how al-Qaeda used the Arab media to spread and promote its ideology.

The new phenomena of freedom of expression and freedom of the press, which have swept the Arab world over the last decade or so, has made some Arab regimes very anxious about the implications of this for their countries. Accordingly, Arab regimes are reluctant to grant transnational media such Al-Jazeera state advertising. They even took a step further to pressurise the private sector not to advertise with Al-Jazeera (Tassopoulos 2007: 8). This was clearly designed to hurt the channel financially and force it to change its broadcasting policies. Some Arab governments took strict measures and closed Al-Jazeera's offices. It is not only Arab regimes which have expressed their discontent against broadcasters such Al-Jazeera: during the Iraq war, the US government adopted very 'repressive measures in its dealing with the media' (Tassopoulos 2007: 10).

Some have linked the lack of freedom of expression to the main goal of preserving Arabic culture. According to Rugh (1987), Arab journalists defend Arabic culture, traditions and norms, and work on preserving Islamic heritage. Based on Rugh's claim, one would envisage a piece of journalism to be stripped of anything negative or offensive about Islamic culture and religion.

Freedom of expression and the law

Media regulation in the Arab world is governed by a set of laws which are passed through parliament. These laws are strictly enforced and journalists who are caught violating them face severe punishments, including imprisonment. The laws are designed to protect governments and states' cultural heritage. Journalists are restricted in their coverage, and in most cases they are not allowed to criticise the government or the state order. For instance, Jordanian law grants the government the power to withdraw licences, issue fines and, in extreme cases, imprison offenders for daring to take on the government. The Emergency Law, which has been imposed by the Egyptian government, gives the authorities the power to close down news agencies, confiscate publications and take severe and decisive measures against 'perpetrators'. Arab governments also passed 'the penal codes to punish persons who encourage violence, defame a head of state, disseminate "false or exaggerated information outside the country that attacks state dignity," or defame a public official' (Amin 2002: 130).

The consequences of these laws for the freedom of expression are visible to everyone. Some governments still maintain control over the content to be broadcast. Journalists will be accustomed to the rhetoric of praising and glorifying the state and the government, and the main victim here is freedom of expression and impartiality in delivering news and information. The other victim is the journalist who finds him/herself caught in the middle. They have to face the option of either taking the government line and sparing the hassle, or speaking their mind and facing harassment and, in some circumstances, imprisonment.

One should not underestimate the power of governments. According to Amin (2002: 131), Arab governments have absolute 'control over the authorization, renewal, and revocation of licenses'. It is these powers that make journalists and media broadcasters alike think twice before publishing anything that can be critical of or unpopular among governments. The limitation of freedom of expression cannot entirely be explained by the restrictive laws passed by Arab governments, however. The economic landscape of the Arab world could also be said to have an impact on the operation of the Arab media. The lack of financial means to modernise and train journalists to adopt a free and fair approach in their reporting made some of the Arab media rely on traditional means of broadcasting. This has clear repercussions on how news and information are imparted to the Arab public.

Freedom of expression and the economic landscape in the Arab world

Most media broadcasters in the Arab world rely on their government for revenue. Most of the newspapers and broadcasters have found themselves at the mercy of their government. Some might risk closure if the government withdrew its advertising revenues, so to keep the flow of these revenues, some newspapers and broadcasters would not transcend the red line drawn by the government. Also, governments use the law of minimum capitalisation to prohibit some newspapers and small broadcasters, especially those that are seen to constitute a challenge to the government, from gaining a licence (Amin 2007: 131). These media outlets know full well that their survival is entirely based on respecting their government's political stance and, where possible, supporting it.

Examples of the control of the media can be found across the Arab world. Take, for instance, Algeria. Private press is banned and the government is in full control of the major printing companies in the country. This means that the fate of the newspapers is in the hands of the government, who can either print their issues or decline them (Amin 2007). The government monopoly over the publication of material makes it difficult for the press to break ranks and publish information that is critical of the government and its policies.

Unlike Algeria, Egypt does allow private media to operate in the country, but the government maintains a complete hegemony over the publishing houses. Like Algeria, newspapers in Egypt found themselves at the mercy of the government. Their material can be censored or rejected at any time.

In Tunisia, the fragile economic situation of most media outlets makes them defenceless against the government control of the market. The same situation is repeated across the Arab world. The government control of resources could be said to be designed to curb freedom of expression in the region. The lack of giant independent media corporations that can sustain themselves independently of government subsidies means that freedom of expression will always be controlled by the government.

The international law with regard to freedom of expression is unequivocal in its support of plurality, protection of the right of freedom of speech. Article 19 of the Universal Declaration of Human Rights, for instance, grants individuals complete freedom to express themselves and impart knowledge without any external restriction or control: 'Everyone has the right to freedom of opinion and expression; this right includes freedom to hold opinions without interference and to seek, receive and impart information and ideas through any media and regardless of frontiers' (United Nations 1948).

These rights are often infringed upon in the Arab world. Most journalists there will find it extremely difficult to apply Article 19 to the letter, as in some contexts the application of the declaration on the ground is not an easy task; it is unquestionably one fraught with dangers and risks. In contexts such as the Middle East, journalists have to assess the impact of their actions on society and government alike, as well as on family unity, culture and belief. These are often considered taboos that should not be broken; however, the new transnational Arab media have already broken the ice with regard to these taboos. This is due to the mushrooming of new media and the development of technologies in the field of information technology. The polarity of media outlets and the advent of the internet have drastically changed the flow of news, and have given it a multi-direction. The availability of information on the internet and satellite channels makes it difficult for Arab governments to control the flow of information. Although this information cannot be accessed by the whole of the Arab public because the majority cannot afford a satellite dish and do not have access to the internet, it is however accessed by many journalists and other media consumers. We should agree with Amin (2007) in thinking that the new technological changes taking place across the globe will make the issue of censorship and control of information a thing of the past. But, there again, we should not lose sight of the fact that in global media market, where competition over market share is increasing by the day, and where objectivity and impartiality are essentials for media survival, both the regional and local media need to adapt to this new culture in order to protect their market and audience. As will be discussed in Chapter 3, Al-Jazeera and Al-Arabiya are two good examples that demonstrate this level of competitiveness both regionally and internationally.

Despite their willingness to relax the code of media practice, some Arab governments will always remain cautious of granting the media complete liberty to operate. This is simply, as Amin (2007) puts it, because they do not trust journalists. For the freedom of the press and media to gain momentum in the Arab world, organisations such as Arab Press Freedom Watch should take their role seriously, and should be 'recognised by the journalists' congresses' (Amin 2007: 133).

The development of network communication in the Arab world

As aforementioned, the Arab world has witnessed a rapid expansion in the development of satellite television and networks. The internet is seen to be a growing medium of communication across the Arab world. Most Arab universities and schools now encourage their students to use the internet for educational purposes. It provides Arab users with the opportunity to search information, socialise through different social networks, and browse the current national news. The internet also provides the opportunity to access international news and information, which is not necessarily compatible with the news and information imparted by the local media. Some Arab users employ the internet to debate issues and express their own opinions on matters related to their own interests. The fact that some use the internet to voice their opinions about the coverage of certain issues on Arab channels is an encouraging prospect.

The popularity of the internet in the Arab world has led to the proliferation of cyberspace usage and encouraged telecommunication companies to offer broadband at reasonable and affordable prices.

Anderson (1997) highlighted two main characteristics of network communication:

> the most striking feature of the internet in this regard is spontaneous, unofficial representation. What this activity marks is an increasingly public, unmoderate (and not infrequently immoderate) representation that traditional participants can join on their own authority and interest plus ability to use the technology. [. . .] By comparison to the asymmetrical arrangements of broadcasting, on the internet barriers to access are only slightly higher for senders than receivers, and those are coming down all over.

Despite the common language and culture, the level of development of information technology in the Arab world varies from one state to another. This is due to the level of education, rate of illiteracy and the financial variables in each country, by which I mean individual and family incomes. In addition to the educational and economic factors, the political willingness to use this medium of communication is at the heart of Arab government policies. The growth in the number of internet users has placed a lot of pressure on Arab governments to have more internet ports.

Although there is an inclination by some Arab countries to use the internet, 4 out of the 15 states identified by Reporters sans frontières (RSF) to be controlling the use of the internet are Arab countries: Libya, Saudi Arabia, Syria and Tunisia (qtd in Hofheinz 2007: 57).

The content and information that should be accessible on the internet remains an issue for some Arab governments, who have resorted to filtering and blocking information and sites that they deem a threat to their people and state. The UAE and Yemen often use SmartFilter software to restrict their citizens' access to undesirable material, such as certain sites and content, and 'to monitor web use from behind proxy servers' (Hofheinz 2007: 57).

Saudi Arabia has a special committee chaired by the ministry of the interior and implemented by the Internet Services Unit (ISU) that monitors access to the internet. The ISU is responsible for blocking content and sites that are in violation of Islamic tradition or national regulations. This includes materials on pornography, drugs and gambling, as well as sites promoting conversion to Christianity (Hofheinz 2007). The ISU even encourages the public to suggest sites which promote materials in violation of the state's traditional norms. Equally, the public are encouraged to ask for sites to be unblocked that the ISU might inadvertently have blocked. 'Keep the net clean' is the slogan used by the ISU to encourage the public to be active in helping getting rid of undesirable material.

The UAE has adopted a similar approach. The internet in the UAE is solely dominated by the state-owned Etisalat, the only provider of internet services in the country. Like Saudi Arabia, the UAE justifies the blocking of sites and content as being 'inconsistent with the country's "political, moral, and religious values" ' (Hofheinz 2007: 58); and, again like Saudi Arabia, it uses the SmartFilter software to filter material on pornography, drugs, gambling and conversion to other religions. The constant fear of losing family values is one reason why the majority favour the filtering practice. The erosion of discipline and respect in some Arab countries is often blamed on the Western culture which is infiltrating Arab homes through means such as the internet.

Syria was the last Arab country to allow its citizens access to the internet. This came about just a year after Bashar al-Assad ascended to the throne. The young president was the founder of the Syrian Computer Society (SCS). However, the internet has been subjected to a rigorous monitoring system, where opposition sites are blocked and media materials are censored: the popular Arabic newspaper, *Al-Hayat*, is blocked, as is *Al-Quds Al-Arabi* (Hofheinz 2007). Violating the network regulation has often led to severe punishment which can amount to months of imprisonment.

The filtering policy is less restrictive in countries such as Bahrain, Qatar and Jordan, however, where filtering has targeted pornographic and political opposition sites. In 2005, Bahrain 'blocked 40 sites without warning. One was Multaqa al-Bahrain, a popular discussion forum established in 1999 that is used by the country's Shiite opposition to organise protests' (Hofheinz 2007: 60). Allowing the opposition a platform to promote their messages and policies is something that some Arab governments will not tolerate; however, the transnational Arabic media have started offering platforms for the opposition to voice their concerns and express their opinions.

Statistics gathered up until 2005 (Hofheinz 2007: 62) indicate that the internet is very popular in Egypt, Morocco and Saudi Arabia. Almost a third of users come from both Egypt and Saudi Arabia, with 4.4 million users and 2.54 million users, respectively. The number of cyber users also increased in Morocco to 4 million by the end of 2005, equivalent to 13 per cent of the population. This is explained by the fact that reasonable and affordable prices are available to cyber users, and internet use has become the norm rather than the exception among the young generation, especially those aged between 20 and 30 years old.

Having discussed the growth of internet users in the Arab world, and the government's control of cyberspace, now let us turn into the impact of the internet on the mobilisation of the Arab public. The inevitable question here is: to what extent does the internet contribute to the mobilisation of the public sphere?

The new means of communication have created interactive

forms for people across the Arab world. These forms 'become very competitive' (Hofheinz 2007: 71) in creating open discussions about matters of concern to the Arab world. These discussions have prompted heated debates that have often led to the breach of widely held taboos in the region. The internet has been used for many purposes and by different groups: it has been used to mobilise the Arab and Muslim public for civic action; it has also been used to raise awareness of national and regional issues of interest to the Arab public. The issue of Palestine, for example, is heavily discussed in cyberspace.

It should be stated here that governments and opposition parties in the Arab world have been very slow to use the internet for their own means. Apart from Egypt, the UAE and Morocco, who have all used the internet to promote their activities, the remainder of the Arab world remains passive as to the employment of the internet. Islamic groups were the first to embrace the internet and use it to promote their agenda. Muslim student associations in both Europe and the United States have intelligently used the internet to draw the world's attention to the 'struggle of Muslim communities in places such as Kashmir, Bosnia, Chechnya and Palestine' (Hofheinz 2007: 72). These groups have used the internet to mobilise the Arab and Muslim public to defend their communities against outsiders. The same approach was adopted by al-Qaeda groups, who have used the internet to disseminate al-Qaeda's messages and threats against the West and as a place to post recordings and information about their activities. This use of the internet has defied the traditional means of communication. Since most of the international media decline to broadcast al-Qaeda's messages because of the threat it poses to the international community, al-Qaeda has resorted to the internet to communicate with its affiliates. The internet is used as the prime channel to mobilise the Arab and Muslim public against the occupation of Palestine, Iraq and Afghanistan. It is also used as a powerful tool to show their ruthless and aggressive actions. This has taken several forms such as the beheading of journalists, and carrying out bold attacks on the US forces in Iraq and Afghanistan. One could conclude from the above discussion that Islamic groups have used the internet to advance their causes and justify their actions.

The impact of this mobilisation process is clearly visible in the rise of the resistance against Western forces in Iraq and Afghanistan. The phenomenon of using the internet as a means to mobilise Iraqis and other Arab nationalists arose in 2004 during the siege of Fallujah (Hofheinz 2007: 72). Many sites were very popular in raising awareness of the American action in Iraq, and in Fallujah in particular. Islammemo.com in particular was very active in mobilising Iraqis and Arab nationalists to support their 'brothers and sisters' stranded in Fallujah. The proliferation of Jihadi sites serves as an indicator of how the internet can be exploited to disseminate messages without having to rely on news channels which, in most cases, do not broadcast full messages.

Other Islamic groups have used both the internet and MSN messages to 'mobilise the electorate on a scale not seen before' (Hofheinz 2007: 73). The Muslim Brotherhood, for instance, used emails and MSN messages in the 2005 election campaign. They used the internet to convey their messages to the electorate, and their website witnessed more traffic than those of the opposition secular parties.

MSN Messenger has a wider reach among the Arab public. Both governments and oppositions have used it to promote their own messages. In March 2005, the Sudanese authorities used Messenger to call for a 'march in protest at the UN's request to the International Criminal Court to investigate allegations of crimes against humanity committed by Sudanese officials' (Hofheinz 2007: 72).

MSN Messenger was not the only tool used to reach out to the majority of the Arab public. The phenomenon of blogging emerged after the decline of the discussion forums. It started in 2004 with Abdallah al-Mihireiri, who translated the word 'blog' into 'al-Mudawwana', and although it failed to gather a collective momentum, it emerged as a favourite individual form of discussion. As a result, an Arab Bloggers' Union was established in 2005. The union held its first annual Best Arab Blog Awards ceremony in the same year, which attracted some media coverage (Hofheinz 2007: 77). Realising the importance of blogging, some internet portals started offering and promoting blogging services, for example Jeeran.com and Albawaba.com. Arab bloggers tend to break with the Arab tradition and adopt a critical perspective of their own regimes as well as of external interference. During the Egyptian elections, for instance, bloggers were very active in filing blogs on the election campaigns and the election results. Some of the traditional media, as well as the Western media, used these blogs as a source of news and information. Blogging in Egypt has produced some good results and gained external recognition through international awards. Manal Alaa's campaign for freedom of expression in Egypt, for instance, won her the RSF special award at the November 2005 Deutsche Welle International Weblog Awards (Hofheinz 2007: 77). The importance of the internet in promoting human rights activities in the Arab world was clearly reiterated by the Human Rights Watch in 2005: 'the Internet's role in strengthening the Egyptian human rights movement is a trend that looks likely to continue.'

Accountability in journalism

The concept of media accountability is one that remains vague in both its definition and functionality. The task of reconciling the freedom of the media with media accountability is a daunting process. Many attempts have been made to marry the two but to no avail. For instance, Thomas Jefferson, in 1805, called for free press and insisted that editors should be 'left to find their punishment in the public indignation'.[3] Jefferson's quotation was a launching pad for discussion about the relationship between freedom and accountability.

Hodges (1986) distinguished quite clearly between accountability and responsibility. He pointed out that it is realistic to have a free and responsible media, but impossible to have a free and accountable media. In the Arab world, it could be concluded that both notions are in their infancy and could take some time to mature. With the emergence of transnational media, the notion of freedom of the press and media accountability is a subject of discussion and debate. The debate takes different forms. The first is the media's role in fulfilling its obligation by broadcasting free, fair and transparent information, which could form public opinion. The second is the media's responsibility to hold governments and opposition accountable for their actions. The notion of media holding governments accountable is fairly a new concept to Arabic culture and the Arab public. The launch of Al-Jazeera has brought some elements of accountability to broadcasting, but this is still a work in progress. The most common practice among the Arab transnational media is to discuss issues and events without pointing the finger at the perpetrators. No individual or organisation should be immune from media's criticism, and media in turn should exercise its power of holding governments accountable for their practices. While Western media has reached a powerful position, and is able to 'make and unmake individuals and institutions, including governments' (Sawant 2003: 17), Arab media has remained the timid broadcaster who gets on well with both governments and giant private organisations. Equally, the notion of accountability does not apply to Arab media. Most of the Arab media is state-run, and therefore accountable to the government but not to the general Arab public. It is about time that the Arab media should be held accountable by the Arab public for its soft reporting, and its association with organisations and governments that are against freedom of expression and the freedom of the press. The media should be held accountable for not doing enough to scrutinise the practices of governments and private organisations, and for any distortion and inaccuracy in its reporting. The Arab audience, like any other international audience, should step into the fray and exercise their right to voice their opinion on any type of information disseminated by the media.

Codes and regulations of the Arab media

Arab national media policies are still heavily influenced by some broad terminology, such as 'national unity' and 'national security'. At times this terminology can serve as a barrier to the free operation of the media, which has been asked to refrain from broadcasting issues related to security and national unity. This undoubtedly undermines the role of the opposition who criticise the governments for their failures (Kraidy and Khalil 2009); the governments can use the pretext of national security and unity to control the content to be aired. Inconsistency in the implementation of certain policies has created confusion about the codes regulating the operation and functionality of the media.

The advent of transnational Arab channels and their coverage of sensitive Arab issues have pushed some Arab governments to call for a new media policy. Egypt led the call for new codes of practice, and in 2008 the Egyptian government proposed a new television law aimed at 'controlling television and video distributed through broadcasting, satellite, cable, the Internet' (Kraidy and Khalil 2009: 140).

It should be noted here, however, that some Arab countries have taken some encouraging measures to relax their media code of practice and regulations. Qatar, for instance, has abolished its ministry of information in an attempt to promote freedom of expression and give the media the liberty needed to broadcast without restriction. Al-Jazeera is a good example, although it came under attack for not being too critical of its host. Syria has also recognised the importance of developing its media in order to be able to convey the Syrian message across the Arab world, and especially to the Lebanese people.

As mentioned previously, in February 2008, Arab ministers endorsed a satellite television charter proposed by Egypt to regulate satellite channels. The charter gives Arab governments the authority to sanction satellite channels which threaten national security, attack Arab leaders or broadcast material deemed socially unacceptable (Kraidy and Khalil 2009: 141). The charter came after satellite channels, such as Al-Jazeera, transcended the borders to criticise and hold Arab governments responsible for domestic and regional issues. But, it was the voice of the Arab public which was active in attacking Arab leaders live on call-in shows. Unused to such a practice, Arab governments felt the need to rein in some of these channels. This became very clear when both the Saudi and Egyptian governments strongly criticised Hezbollah for kidnapping two Israeli soldiers, claiming that this exposed Lebanon to another conflict. Some Arab viewers were discontented with the Saudi and Egyptian move, and took to the air to express their strong criticism of both governments.

Some Arab countries did not sign up for the charter. They opposed it on the grounds that the new charter conflicted with their own national laws. Lebanon, for example, regards it as a guide rather than as a binding law that should be strictly implemented. Journalists opposed the charter altogether, expressing their fear that the new law will limit their freedom of expression and silence those voices that are critical of the US and Israel in the media (Kraidy and Khalil 2009: 143).

Conclusion

This chapter has provided a comprehensive review of the development of the Arab media, both print and audio-visual. Although the Arab media has developed substantially over the last decade or so, its progress may be regarded as slow and often impeded by social, cultural and political factors. The economic factor remains the strongest, however: most of the Arab media lacks the resources to provide strong and reliable coverage of events. Its coverage is often marred by inaccuracies or accusations of supporting regional governments.

The high percentage of illiteracy in the Arab world has been identified as a major factor for the slow development of print media, but it is the political factor that has had the greatest impact on the operation of the Arab media. The strict code of media practice in some Arab countries means that the media exercises little freedom of expression. The control of the dissemination of information by some Arab governments means that the media has little power to have any impact on the government and the public. The emergence of transnational Arab media, however, could be said to have made a difference to the genre of broadcast existing in the Arab world. This media has broken widely held taboos, such as the concept of governance, religion and women. It should be wholeheartedly applauded for its bold move to, at least partially, hold governments accountable for some of their practices across the Arab world.

The notion of media accountability is still in its infancy in the Arab world. The media is still learning how to exert more pressure on Arab governments and hold them accountable for their action in the region; equally, the Arab public should learn how to hold media accountable for either its failure to hold governments accountable, or for its negligence in dealing with sensitive Arab issues.

The proliferation of the Arab media over the last decade and global competition have had a great impact on the functionality of transnational Arab media. This global impact will be assessed in the next chapter.

Chapter 2

Globalisation, Democracy and the Arab Media

Definition of globalisation

Before we embark on any discussion of the relationship between globalisation and democracy on the one hand, and the impact of globalisation on the Arab media on the other, we need first to provide a definition of globalisation. Al-Jabri (2002: 134 in Mellor 2007: 12) defined globalisation as:

> a world without a nation-state, or without a nation and without a state. It is a world of corporations and networks; a world of subjects or 'doers', those in control, and objects of consumption imposed on them, be it the consumption of food, drinks, canned products, images, data, movement and even silence. Cyberspace has become the new nation . . . it is the space which is made by the communication networks to encompass economics, politics, and culture.

One aspect of globalisation which has become apparent over the last decade or so is the entertainment sector (films, music and literature). Unlike other sectors which may be domesticated to reflect local culture and layout, the entertainment sector poses itself as a global complete package (Hafez 2007). Hafez refers to the entertainment industry as the largest capital film makers have. It has a global aspect that has been welcome across the world.

Hafez (2007) paints quite a clear picture of international reporting and how it unifies people across the globe. His example of sporting activities such as the Olympic Games and football illustrates quite well how all broadcasters unite to transmit these international events across the world. During the football World Cup event, the world appears to be a small village unified beyond national and cultural diversity by a sporting activity. At times, however, international broadcasting can often be moulded by national viewpoints and stereotypes (Hafez 2007). A good example of this is the international media's coverage of conflicts, which is often marred by stereotypical references against the parties involved in the conflict. The aftermath of 9/11 saw the American media rally behind their government and they started using approaches such as 'us' and 'them' (see Chapter 4). At a time when the media should question government policy, we saw some of the American media trying to rally behind the government. According to Hafez (2007: 41) 'American television companies became the fount of political slogans urging the nation to unite and support President George W. Bush.' Hafez has also mentions the reaction of the German media to the events of 9/11. Their coverage seemed to link the violent acts with Islam; for example, the magazine *Die Woche* considered Islam as the enemy in one of its articles.

According to Mellor (2007) there is a consensus among both Western and Arab scholars that globalisation means the 'commodification of culture' which might lead to the loss or damage of the authentic fabric. It is this fear of losing one's identity and culture that makes some consider globalisation a threat to their own existence.

'For any media to be considered "global", they must be able to: transcend nation-state boundaries and language communities' (Barker 2000). It is evident from Barker's statement that there are two elements of crucial importance for any media to achieve the status of global impact: language and the ability to broadcast beyond national borders. The language barrier remains one of the main challenges for the international media to overcome if it is to achieve global impact; however, there are some examples of media which have had an influence on the global public through their hegemonic coverage of certain events. CNN's coverage of the first

Gulf War, for instance, made the channel a recognised face the world over. Although CNN's coverage was in English, many international media translated it into the language appropriate to their audience. It could be argued, therefore, that CNN has had an indirect impact on the global audience since its coverage was transferred through the medium of translation. CNN's impact goes beyond its temporary coverage of the 1991 Gulf War, though, as it has made a name for itself by not shying away from covering controversial events and has become a recognised face across the globe. The question to be posed here, however, is: can any channel that achieves temporary influence on the global public sphere be categorised as a global media outlet? A clear answer to this question would lead us to examine Al-Jazeera's dominant coverage of the war on Afghanistan, and whether this coverage qualifies the channel to claim a global impact. In a similar way to CNN, Al-Jazeera had a short-lived hegemony over the coverage of the war on Afghanistan. As mentioned in Chapter 3, the channel's logo and broadcasting messages have been aired globally through the medium of translation, and without a doubt, it has gained fame and popularity across the world. The international media had to rely on Al-Jazeera for news and information coming from Afghanistan, thus the channel became internationally recognised and its reporters became familiar faces across the globe. Unlike CNN, however, Al-Jazeera's moment of fame came to an abrupt end after the Taliban government was ousted by American forces. The global impact of Al-Jazeera came in the aftermath of the war, when al-Qaeda chose Al-Jazeera for airing their recorded messages. The channel once again took to the international stage, but its impact on the international scene was limited this time, and largely restricted to the Arab public sphere. Although the channel aspires to have global influence, there are number of factors that constitute a hindrance to its aspirations, including 'Restrictive state policies [. . .] and a lack of acceptance of new media by state authorities' (Kirchner 2001: 137).

Mellor (2007) considers the media as the bridge to globalisation because it is used as a route 'to facilitate the agents' movement to and from other fields while serving as a communicative platform to disseminate the norms and rules that restrain these movements' (2007: 19). The Arab media illustrates well how the media can serve as a platform to circulate and promote norms that are often considered a threat to the foundations of society. Numerous programmes such as *Star Academy* and *al-Itijah al-Mu'akiss* could be seen as serving to promote Western culture by trying to create an open society in the fields of art and politics. *Star Academy*, which is modelled on the famous British programmes *The X Factor* and *Britain's Got Talent*, is regarded by some critics as promoting Western youth culture, where young women are seen to mix with young men, and where feelings of affection and love are aired unedited and uncensored. *al-Itijah al-Mu'akiss* is also seen as adopting a Western style by creating open and uncontrolled debate, mainly in the field of politics. Through this approach, the Arab media has sought to 'connect people and accentuate their belonging to one unified imagined community while enabling their movement across diverse and unrelated fields, which threatens the foundation of this community' (Mellor 2007: 19).

The above programmes can be considered as a new medium through which the Arab public is introduced to a new, different culture and lifestyle. The participation of the Arab public in such programmes through numerous call-in shows gives the participants a sense of confidence and fame, though only temporarily. These practices have become global because they are widely practised by other media outlets and other people from different cultures.

While most Arab states' media still pursue a traditional broadcasting line, which ensures that Arab culture, identity and language are safeguarded, transnational Arab media such as Al-Jazeera and Al-Arabiya have taken a completely different approach in their broadcasting, an approach based on openness and interaction with the external world through different broadcasting activities. The main intention is to create a global Arab public.

The competition to extend their hegemony beyond their national borders has led some Western media to launch either new channels in Arabic to promote their policies and points of views, or new websites containing new material in Arabic. Following its success, CNN, for instance, launched a website in Arabic. Other news organisations have followed suit (Mellor 2007: 52). On 27 July 2003, CNBC Arabiya was launched, and in 2007, the BBC launched BBC Arabic. These new channels and websites are designed to explain British and American views and values to the Arab public. Al-Jazeera followed the same strategy and launched its channel in English. The launch of Al-Jazeera English came after the astounding success of the channel in its coverage of the war on Afghanistan.

The desire to have an impact on the global audience has triggered many Western and Arab governments, as well as private organisations, to launch their own websites and channels in order to communicate their policies to a wider audience. In the Arab world, the Arab media has found itself under fierce competition from Western channels which have launched their own Arabic version. In response to this, the Arab media has extended its reach to the Arab public beyond national geographic boundaries. Abu Dhabi, for instance, has upgraded its programmes and news coverage and become a key player in the Arab media market. Al-Arabiya was launched to compete for the Arab audience, and Al-Hurra was launched to explain the US government's policies to the Arab public.

Since 1996, Al-Jazeera Arabic has competed fiercely with the Arab local media for a greater share of the Arabic market. Its broadcasting style, which has sparked controversial debates on numerous occasions, has earned the channel its popularity on the Arab street, and made it one of the most watched satellite channels in the Arab world. It has invaded living rooms from Morocco to Syria. This unprecedented success has been attributed to the lack of competition in the Arab media market; however, even at a time when new Arab channels – the US-backed Al-Hurra, and Al-Arabiya – came on the scene, Al-Jazeera remained the most favoured and the leading channel in the Arab world.

Al-Jazeera Arabic's popularity caught observers and media critics by surprise, especially during the war on Afghanistan. Its monopoly over the coverage of the war made the channel one of the most recognisable brands globally. Yet, its international audience could not follow its coverage because of the language barrier. This led to the launch of Al-Jazeera English, which pledged to reach new markets and attract a new audience beyond the social and cultural borders of the Arab world; a move that was designed to attract a wider audience from the English-speaking world. This strategy, which is called 'glocalisation', has been implemented by many international channels such as BBC World, CNN International and Al-Jazeera English (Hahn 2007). The BBC, for instance, has launched an Arabic-language satellite television news channel to cater for the local Arab audience; and CNN launched an Arabic-language website to ensure that its news reports are disseminated to the Arab public. In 2003, the US government launched its channel Al-Hurra, with the aim of promoting freedom and democracy in the region. Pattiz summarises Al-Hurra's mission, saying 'the station's respect for its audience and message of personal empowerment is in stark contrast to the messages of victimisation put out by the major government controlled television channels in the region' (Pattiz 2004: 79).

Realising the significant role of media in winning hearts and minds, the US government felt the urgent need to reach out to the Arab public through an Arabic-sponsored channel.

The US government's endeavour to win over Arab hearts and minds was evident in its launch of Radio Sawa, which came as a replacement to Voice of America Arabic. Radio Sawa is mainly directed at the Arab youth generation, therefore its programmes are tailor made to suit and 75 per cent of its programming comprises music, in both Arabic and English. The American Board of Broadcasting Governors justified this move by referring to the fact that half of the Middle Eastern population is under the age of 35 years. This strategy was intended to mobilise the Arab public, in the same way as Voice of America had mobilised mass movements in Poland and Eastern Europe during the Second World War (Pattiz 2004).

Al-Jazeera English is not alone in its quest to attract a global audience. Germany's international broadcaster Deutsche Welle (DW), for example, started subtitling its programmes in Arabic. Reaching a global media market after the events of September 2001 became a priority for most governments and media organisations; the global media is often regarded as the best means of global communication and understanding.

In addition to establishing a line of communication worldwide, some governments' media have been used to promote their governments' values and beliefs to an international audience.

France, for example, launched its joint public–private television news network, France 24, aimed at spreading French views and values (Sakr 2007: 1). Equally, Russia launched its English channel, Russia Today, to promote news from a Russian perspective. The proliferation of international media reflects the global endeavour of organisations and governments to make their voices heard, and perhaps have an influence on the international public sphere.

The desire to win the global audience's hearts and minds is at the heart of every channel, and Al-Jazeera English is no exception. Competition among channels for global recognition has made the world a small village, where different cultures conquer our living rooms daily. This means that different social values, political culture and communication systems are aired by different channels to their target audiences (Hahn 2007). This diversity in terms of broadcasting is not without its ramifications. According to Hahn (2007), the media can at times contribute to creating intercultural friction. The decision of some European media to reprint offensive caricatures of the Prophet Mohammed, despite the indignation of the Arab media, is a clear example of this type of intercultural friction (Hahn 2007). The same can be said of the choice of language by broadcasters. Pro-Israeli media would describe the killing of Palestinian activists as 'target killing', while some Arab media would refer to it as 'assassination'. What is considered as a 'terrorist' by some media outlets can be seen as a 'freedom fighter' in the eyes of others.

Hahn (2007: 21–2) attributed intercultural friction to 'the political power relations in international relations and their implications for communication'. The challenge facing the international media today is its stance as a global broadcaster in the face of powerful nations. Will it subscribe to the policies of powerful nations, or will it adopt a critical perspective towards their policies? After 9/11, for instance, the American media was torn between adopting a patriotic stance and airing independent and balanced reports. The American President George W. Bush's famous statement, 'you are either with us or against us', in the aftermath of the atrocious events of September 2001, put some media outlets in an awkward position. Going against the US government's official line would risk them being isolated and tarnished as unpatriotic. This led some of the American and international media to follow the same line as the US government by adopting the phrase 'war on terror', without even questioning the motives behind it.

Many of the Western media strive to represent the global audience, and the Arab media is no exception. The following section focuses on Al-Jazeera English and its endeavour to make a global impact on the non-Arabic audience.

Al-Jazeera English: a global discourse

Al-Jazeera's catchphrases and motto were selected to reflect the ambitious aims and objectives of this infant channel. 'Every side', 'every angle' and 'fearless journalism' are the most frequent catchphrases used in its promotion. They reflect the 'comprehensive' approach to broadcasting that Al-Jazeera intends to follow, or aspires to achieve; an approach which, it claims, will place freedom of expression, transparency and fairness at the heart of its journalistic practices. The catchphrases are derived from Al-Jazeera's desire to reverse the flow of news from the South to the North. This discourse of 'global' mission emanates from Al-Jazeera's salient aims to bring the East and West together and to cover stories from remote corners of Africa and Asia; however, critics have expressed their reservation about the balance of news from both South and North. Lawrence Pintak, Director of the Adham Center for Electronic Journalism at the American University in Cairo, noted that because of the channel's focus on the South, the 'North ceased to exist' in the first day of the channel's coverage.

Al-Jazeera's liberal discourse practices characterise it as one of the most radical channels in the Middle East. According to Atton (2002b: 495), radical media are described by their 'attempt to free themselves from the power of government, the state and other dominant institutions and practices'. Al-Jazeera English can be characterised as radical because of its agenda of providing free and balanced coverage away from the influence of governments or organisations inside and outside the Middle East. Its discourse tends to shift away from the traditional Middle Eastern media discourse, which is based on safeguarding culture and defending the social norms and traditions of the region. Such a shift is an indicator of Al-Jazeera's aims of appealing to a global audience beyond Middle Eastern borders. This is in line with its 'global mission' of broadcasting. Like its Arabic sister, Al-Jazeera English's aim is to empower the powerless and give voice to the voiceless across the globe. Its decision to focus on the South is part of its agenda of bringing 'neglected and uncovered stories' to our newsrooms. Its focus on ordinary people is evidently manifested in Riz Khan's programme, *Street Talk*, where ordinary people are given the freedom to act as amateur journalists and present accounts of ordinary people. Based on Atton's definition of radical media referred to above, Al-Jazeera English fits well within this category.

Another aspect of radical media is 'native reporting' (Atton 2002b). Al-Jazeera's journalists come from forty-five nations, making it one of the most diverse channels in the world. The selection and positioning of native reporters has been adopted to attract an audience who relate to its journalists and reporters. The appointment and stationing of David Frost in London, for instance, could be said to have been done to attract the British audience who are familiar with this presenter. The same could be said about David Marsh, a former employee of Al-Jazeera, and Riz Khan, the popular faces of American media. Unlike non-native journalists, native reporters can have the advantage of having easy access to the community in which they live. A good illustration is Al-Jazeera English's programme *Inside Iraq*, which is hosted by an Arab native speaker who uses his language and cultural background to get the assistance and support needed from the community for his programme, such as interviewing ordinary people using their language, and accessing institutions. 'Inside Iraq' is one of the tangible examples of how Al-Jazeera English is using the technique of 'native reporting' to access communities and cover stories from within, a task that non-native journalists might find fraught with dangers because of security issues. Addressing communities in languages that relate to them most not only helps journalists to compose good reports, but often helps them to establish a channel of communication with these communities which will ensure support and assistance in future reporting, should the reporter decided to go back to that community. Al-Jazeera English seems to be aware of the significance of this technique in compiling reports and attracting viewers. Although these practices are not new to modern journalism, Al-Jazeera seems to implement them in most of its reporting zones.

Perhaps the most striking feature about Al-Jazeera English's broadcasting is its access to remote areas. This enables its journalists to offer alternative news reports to those of the mainstream media. But can this qualify Al-Jazeera English to be characterised as 'alternative media' or a global media channel?

According to Iskandar (2006), an alternative media is the one that 'provides representations of issues and events that are in opposition to the portrayals of the same issues and events in the mainstream media'. Iskandar's definition encompasses some of Al-Jazeera's aims and objectives manifested in highlighting issues in the South, which are not covered by the mainstream Western media. Its global discourse practices are reflected in the following statement made by Alan Fisher, Al-Jazeera's Europe correspondent: 'we will take a global view, rather than looking at things from a purely Western perspective' (G. Adams 2006).

While Fisher focused on the global mission of Al-Jazeera, his colleague, Charlie Courtauld, placed great emphasis on Al-Jazeera's independence from any interference by its sponsors. He was quoted in *The Canberra Times* as having said that Al-Jazeera English is 'an independent production and we have full editorial control. That is very important, because it is undeniable that some people have strong views about Al-Jazeera which are generally based on second-hand info, because they don't speak Arabic.'[1]

Al-Jazeera English's independence has also been reflected in its language code of practice. Its journalists and reporters refer to Iraqi fighters, for instance, as 'guerrillas' and not 'terrorists' as portrayed in the Western media. The term 'target killing', which is widely used by mainstream media in describing Israel's killing of Palestinian activists, is often replaced with the term 'killing'.

Despite its competition with giant channels such as the BBC, CNN and Fox News, Al-Jazeera's press release, a year after its launch, indicated that the channel attracted a global viewer footprint of 100 million homes. Abdullah Al Najjar, commercial director of Al-Jazeera Network, commented on Al-Jazeera's achievement a year on, saying 'in just one year, Al Jazeera English has exceeded our wildest expectations in terms of its global carriage'.[2]

Prior to Al-Jazeera's launch, most Western journalists and critics had predicted that Al-Jazeera would find it extremely difficult to compete with the giant Western media corporations. A year after its launch, however, reports indicated that Al-Jazeera had passed its first test with flying colours. It scored highly in certain departments such as programming, but achieved low scores in its news reporting and its website. This small success motivated Al-Jazeera's management team to find distributors who would agree to carry it in the United States.

The appointment of veteran Phil Lawrie as director of global distribution was designed to promote Al-Jazeera in the United States, India and China. It is worth mentioning here that Al-Jazeera is already accessible online and it is reported that up to 60 per cent of its hits are coming from the United States.[3] According to Al-Jazeera's management team, this is a sign that viewers in America are growing to like the channel. Despite being rejected by US providers, Al-Jazeera's profile was boosted when Israel's largest cable network, HOT, decided to replace CNN with Al-Jazeera English. Yossi Lubaton, the company's vice president of marketing, justified this move, saying 'most of the internationally famous news channels – Sky News, the BBC and Fox – for all of them the cost is significantly lower than CNN. [The move] to introduce Al-Jazeera in English comes at a much lower cost than CNN.'[4]

Lubaton considered the replacement to be financially motivated, and not based on the quality of CNN's performance or the quality of its programmes. Some have regarded this move as compromising quality. Professor Tamar Liebes, head of the Hebrew University's communications department, considered the replacement a 'joke', adding that most of Israelis will not 'trust Al-Jazeera's coverage of international affairs'. Comparing Al-Jazeera with CNN, Liebes said that 'whatever functions CNN performed, none of them will be performed by Al-Jazeera. It's a whole different kind of person who will watch.'[5]

Liebes was not alone in questioning the integrity of the channel. In an article in *The Guardian* newspaper, Holmwood (2008) discussed how some of Al-Jazeera's employees were discontented with the working environment. He reported that the English channel's rolling services 'cost so much to set up that they are now cutting costs at the expense of quality and quantity'. In the same article, Holmwood referred to the low morale among staff. He quoted a source as saying that 'some people worked very hard to produce a channel but there is no recognition whatsoever'.

In addition to this, Al-Jazeera is locked in a dispute with a former employee, Jo Burgin, who filed a case against Al-Jazeera for sex, race and religious discrimination; an accusation which Al-Jazeera's head of media relations, Satnam Matharu, rejected, emphasising 'Al-Jazeera's mission and vision has always been based on the values of human dignity, equality, and diversity. This applies not only to our coverage but also to our organization.'[6]

The dispute has generated many questions with regard to Al-Jazeera's international status. Some have questioned whether it will be able to rise to the high level of international corporations, and compete with internationally renowned media outlets on a global scale.

Global media and the public sphere

Before we dwell on any discussion of the relationship and impact of the global media on the public sphere, I believe it is appropriate to provide a definition of the public sphere. Habermas defines the public sphere as a 'sphere which mediates between society and state, in which the public organizes itself as the bearer of public opinion' (Khatib 2007: 30). The public sphere is seen as a space where ideas and opinions are discussed and channelled in an organised way that might have a 'limiting impact on the state' (Price 1995: 25). In the context of the Arab world, the Arab public has yet to reach the level of having an impact on the state and government, and this is due to the lack of organisation, a pivotal element of Habermas's theory of the public sphere. In the Arab world, the Arab public is organised or galvanised through the 'visual-image effect', where broadcast images, be it of Palestinians, Iraqis or other fellow Arabs and Muslims, serve as a rallying factor to support Arab and Muslim causes. By broadcasting these images, the Arab media have sought to covertly mobilise the Arab public. This reinforces Pierre Bourdieu's saying that the 'power to show is also a power to mobilize' (qtd in Khatib 2007: 30).

Two dominant forces have emerged over the last few years in the Arab world: the media which seek to mobilise and influence the public to take action and adopt an active role, and Arab governments who work to keep the public under tight control. When the Arab public starts demonstrating an active role, Arab governments often rush in to introduce pacifying reforms to subdue feelings of discontent among the Arab public. We have seen, for instance, how most Arab governments allowed demonstrations to be held in public during the 2009 Israeli offensive on Gaza. This strategy was adopted to show the Arab governments' solidarity with the Palestinians, but in real terms, some of these governments were very slow to respond to the plight of the Palestinians and their needs. Although some eventually did, the action was considered too little and too late to prevent the suffering of Palestinians living in Gaza.

Coleman and Ross (2010: 21) describe the public space as a 'set of spatial relations within which social actions take place. Public space should not be understood in a narrowly topological sense, as a physically dimensional place, but as a social configuration comprising practiced and experienced relationships of interaction'

Coleman and Ross (2010) refer to the process of interaction and social action that takes place among citizens. This interaction is not confined to a certain space, but it is an open interaction among the citizens of the world. To create this open interaction, we need means of communication that break down the barriers of individual states and cultures. The Arab transnational media could be cited here to demonstrate how it has created social interaction among the Arab public. The television channels' entertainment shows and political programmes have created social discussion and debate among the citizens of the Arab world. But this would not have taken place were it not for the shared language and culture. Here, I am not advocating Habermas's concept that the public is a homogeneous entity, a concept that could exclude foreigners and indigenous populations, but I am arguing that a common language could contribute to establishing an 'experienced social interaction'.

As mentioned above, Habermas considers the public sphere not only as a form of mediation between the society and state, but as 'an arena for civil interaction and rational discussion' (Mellor 2007: 120). Habermas's notion of public sphere has been the main focus of researchers and thinkers who have constantly argued in favour of a global public sphere. Ingrid Volkmer argued that the public sphere 'has become an extra-societal global sphere of mediation particularly enhanced by the internet' (qtd in Mellor 2007: 120). The internet has become a new weapon in the hands of activists to mobilise the global public, and to raise awareness of their agenda. The demonstrations and protests in Iran following the dispute over the fairness of the 2009 Iranian presidential elections were mobilised through online social networking sites such as Facebook, Twitter and MSN Messenger. The information posted on Facebook or on any other online social network is shared by a global audience inside and outside Iran. The internet has also been used by anti-war activists as a tool to mobilise global supporters and organise worldwide demonstrations. Organisations such as al-Qaeda have used the internet for their own ends, often communicating their messages via the internet to a larger audience. The internet is not the only media tool that has been used to promote activities, however; local and international media have also contributed widely to creating this global public sphere. The international media's desire to attract a global audience has helped in creating a global public sphere.

Hjarvard, however, argues that opinion formation 'is still very much tied to the level of national political institutions' (qtd in Mellor 2007: 120–1). He argues against the assumption that the public sphere is globally mobilised. Mellor (2007), on the other hand, acknowledges that there is greater interconnectedness among world nations through transnational media. This interconnectedness has created a new global public sphere. The Arab public sphere has been widely affected, and as a consequence a new Arab public sphere has emerged. Lynch (2006: 21) defines it as an 'expanding universe of Arabs able and willing to engage in public arguments about political issues'. The new Arab public is shaped by the wide range of existing transnational channels. It is defined by its identity and sense of belonging, and not tied to national geographical borders (Lynch 2006). The fact that they share a common language and news agenda has made the Arab public strong and unified. But there are other unifying factors that continue to form Arab public opinions. According to Lynch (2006), foreign policy, religious identity and national dignity continue to form Arab opinion and create debate and discussion in the Arab public sphere, debate often channelled through the transnational media and online forums. The nature of these debates and public opinion is mostly 'liberal and permissive', given that these opinions most likely originate from cities, where there is a high rate of literacy and educated people (Lynch 2006).

Apart from these factors, one should not overlook the fact that the new Arab generation, most of whom are young and Westernised, tend to adopt a Western approach to everything, including dress code, music and language. Online forums reflect this new direction of Arab youth, which is a new, fearless generation that does not shy away from expressing their opinions or making their voices heard. A typical example of this is the active role of readers on Al-Jazeera's online forums, where entries reflect different views about all aspects of Arab society. The impact of these opinions on Arab government and society is evidently manifested in the Tunisian and Egyptian revolutions, which have led to the ousting of Ben Ali and Hosni Mubarak. The public action has ushered in a new era and a change to both government and society.

One feature that characterises Arab opinion is that it does not bow to external pressure and remains resistant to any external influence (Lynch 2006). Such resistance reflects the Arab public's ability to filter information and differentiate between what is influential and what is non-influential. But when it comes to the Arab media, it can be argued that it has managed, on numerous occasions, to mobilise public opinion. The Arab public took to the street in protest against the occupation of Iraq, and this was largely prompted by Al-Jazeera's live coverage of events in Iraq. The same applies to the channel's coverage of Palestinian issues, which has sparked large protests across the Arab world in support of Palestinians.

The Arab media have played a salient role in creating a public sphere where information is widely shared and debated. The transnational media has created a space for discussion and debate, especially when it comes to matters of importance to the Arab public. The wide range of programmes offered by the Arab media has encouraged debate and rational criticism, which has been missing for so long in the Arab public sphere. The ability to discuss controversial issues live on air with passionate beliefs reflects not only audiences' public engagement with issues of most importance to them, but their ability and willingness to accommodate and respect other views and opinions. This is partly because some of the public have grown accustomed to different views being aired on transnational and international media. I would argue here that tolerating other opinions is a healthy phenomenon and a sign that the new Arab public has moved a long way towards embracing other views. The recent uprisings and revolutions across the Arab world have demonstrated that the Arab public has matured and can start producing results similar to those we witnessed in Eastern Europe around 1989. One could argue that the new Arab public has all necessary ingredients of becoming very influential: it has passion, enthusiasm and common features such as language, identity and culture.

The different political orientations of the Arab public should be emphasised here. The rich discussion and often heated debate about the vision and direction of the Arab states reflect clearly the polarised views which spring from different schools of thought. The Arab public is often aware that any division in opinions could be exploited by external forces deemed hostile to the Arab world, however; as a consequence, it avoids any discussion that could deepen such a division and exacerbate the situation (Lynch 2006).

The development of the Arab public is inextricably linked to the development of the Arab media. The Arab public sphere has been heavily influenced by the Arab media. In the 1950s, the Voice of the Arabs radio station contributed to forming an Arab public fully aware of its Arab nationalism. Voice of the Arabs was used to mobilise the Arab public to rise against its governments and imperialism. Not only did it succeed in influencing the Arab public, but it managed to create, and for the first time, an Arab public that was willing to take action and protest against its governments. Yemen and Iraq are obvious examples of this. According to Lynch (2006: 36), through its broadcasting, Voice of the Arabs managed to form an 'emotional, angry rhetoric aimed at energizing dangerous mobs'. Gamal Abdel Nasser used Voice of the Arabs to unify the Arab public under the banner of one nation, one language and one public. Disillusioned with its own governments and with the colonial powers, the Arab public responded emotionally to his call and embraced his new ideas. Abdel Nasser successfully created a transnational Arab radio station and a transnational Arab public. Although subsequent wars damaged its credibility, Abdel Nasser continued to enjoy popularity and the support of the Arab public. His speeches, which resonated across the Arab world, made his a voice recognised for eloquence and an excellent command of the Arabic language. Nasser's popularity and his transnational messages raised suspicion among other Arab governments, however, who became concerned that his broadcasts were eroding public support for them and mobilising their citizens against them. To confront Nasser's move, some Arab regimes took drastic measures to ensure total state control over the media (Lynch 2006). This reduced the Arab public's support for Nasser and his ideas of Arab nationalism. The Arab public came under a series of monitoring rules and regulations that restricted their movements, debate and access to transnational media. The state media was used to domesticate the Arab public by focusing on national issues, rather than on regional matters that were used by Nasser to appeal to the Arab public. The state became very active in cracking down on any media that crossed its red lines. The strict measures adopted by some Arab governments against media, however, had a devastating effect on the operation of the media in Arab countries, as many newspapers and professional journalists relocated to Europe to ensure freedom of expression and free dissemination of information (Lynch 2006). Despite this, tight control over the borders meant that migrated media news and information was kept away from the Arab states. The Arab public turned to foreign sources for news such as BBC Arabic service, Radio Monte Carlo and Voice of America Arabic (Lynch 2006). London and Paris were the most popular destinations for the operation of migrating media.

The 1970s and 1980s was difficult period for the Arab media. It was heavily monitored and controlled, which in turn has a clear impact on the Arab public's access to news and information. The dearth of information in the national media meant that the Arab public was not fully informed about what was going on regionally. Debate and discussion was limited to national and domestic issues. The 1990s, by contrast, heralded a new era for the Arab media and Arab public. The launch of Al-Jazeera has changed the Arab broadcasting landscape. Its Western broadcasting approach meant that no topic would be spared and no government would be immune to its criticism. Its open programmes have given the Arab public the opportunity to voice concerns without fear. I would argue here that Al-Jazeera has contributed to the revival of the active, emotional Arab public through its focus on Arab issues. Other Arab media have followed suit. The competition among the Arab media to win over the Arab public has not only strengthened the Arab public, but made it one of the most well-informed. Reliance on state channels has become history as most Arab audiences tune in to watch transnational channels.

Two main issues struck me as focal when dealing with the Arab media and the Arab public. The first is that the Arab public could not exist in isolation from the Arab media. The Arab media remains the oxygen of the Arab public; Arab people are informed and mobilised by this media. Secondly, a new culture of awareness, accountability and responsibility among the Arab public has created a new culture of communication and interaction between the media and the public. The Arab public has become more aware than ever of its role in changing society. The focus of the new media on politics and current affairs in the Arab world has lessened the Arab public's interest in the *musalsalats* and entertainment shows which used to be offered by Lebanese and Egyptian channels (Lynch 2006). According to Lynch (2006: 41), credit should be given to 'Al-Jazeera's prioritisation of politics and its remarkable success in initiating a region-wide public discourse that quickly reached an incredibly widespread and diverse audience'. Indeed, although it has its pitfalls and shortcomings, Al-Jazeera, like Voice of the Arabs, could be said to have played a great role in shaping the new Arab public. Al-Jazeera is not alone in contributing to the formation of the new public, however; Al-Arabiya, Al-Jazeera's new rival, could also be said to have made a contribution. Lynch (2006: 43) holds a different view and considers the launch of Al-Arabiya an attempt 'to strip the satellite television stations of their public sphere qualities and return them to a more conventional news media'. One can sympathise with Lynch's statement that some of the satellite channels have been launched to promote governments' policies and domestic activities, but the move could also have a positive side to it. The proliferation of the media could lead to fierce competition and subsequently to fair and transparent broadcasting. In response to the emerging active role of the Arab public, local and national media have started for the first time to adopt a more liberal approach in their coverage. By doing so, they have found in the Arab public an interactive partner who responds quite emotionally to national and regional matters. Although the Arabic public's level of response and engagement could be regarded as satisfactory, its structure and organisation are still not developed to the level that would make it a strong entity that could have some influence on Arab governments. The fact that its action is prompted by the media and its response is limited to the national level is an example that the structural fabric of the public is lacking. Lynch (2006) argues that due to the 'weak' position of the Arab public, it has been unable to translate its action into tangible political outcomes. This lack of political outcomes can be traced back to the lack of organisation and leadership. In the absence of leadership and agenda, it is difficult to envisage the Arab public as a conduit for reform and change (Lynch 2006). However, the 2011 development in the Arab world has caught everyone by surprise. The Egyptian and Tunisian revolutions, along with uprisings and protests across the Arab world, have shown – contrary to what Lynch has referred to – that the Arab public are capable of making drastic changes, even in the absence of leadership. People power can have a big impact on both political systems and societies.

The Arab media as a global practice

In a section entitled 'Hybridity in Arab media', Mellor (2007) starts off by defining hybridity as a result of blending different cultural signs into one. This practice is prevalent in the Arab media, where Western cultural signs are mixed with Arabic signs. The programme *Star Academy* is just one example of how contestants adopted a Western style in their performances. By being a hybrid, the Arab media aimed at striking a balance between what is often called 'moderate' and 'traditionalist'. The new Arab media's flexibility and willingness to merge different cultural signs into one is in stark contrast with the traditional media whose main objective is to safeguard Arabic culture and identity.

The new Arab media practice could be seen to bridge the existing gaps between different cultures, and promote harmony between different people. It also demonstrates that the universality and superiority of one culture over the other is a rhetoric that should be overcome. I would argue that the new Arab media practice has contributed to the emergence of a tolerant, open-minded Arab public that is willing to accommodate different cultural signs and accept different views. The flexibility of the media has created a flexible Arab public. The new Arab media has played the role of instructor. It has invited the Arab public to assess and evaluate other cultural signs before embracing them. Some consider the new media's approach as a 'threat to the indigenous culture and tradition, and a triumph of one dominant culture', however (M. Adams 2006, cited in Mellor 2007: 123).

The active role of the public

In her analysis of the coverage of the aftermath of the assassination of Rafiq Hariri, especially the demonstrations in the centre of Beirut, Khatib (2007) argued that what struck her is not the role of media in covering the protest live to the Lebanese people, but the ability of the Lebanese public to use the television to serve their own agenda. Some of the Lebanese media, especially the anti-Syrian media, sought to mobilise the Lebanese and Arab public against the Syrian government. The same could be said of the demonstrators who tried to convey their anti-Syrian sentiments through national and transnational media. The Lebanese case is just one example of how the Arab public has started using the media to advance its own cause. What happened at the centre of Beirut was disseminated across the Arab world. But, this particular incident has divided the Arab public. There were those who supported the protests and expressed the same anti-Syrian feelings, and those who voiced their support for the Syrians' presence in Lebanon. The sectarian divide in Lebanon is reflected in the polarised opinions across the Arab public. In contrast to this polarisation of opinion reflected by the Lebanese incident, the coverage of the 2006 conflict between Hezbollah and Israel brought the Arab public together in support of Hezbollah.

An example of the role of the media in creating debate among the Arab public is the popular *Star Academy* programme, aired by a satellite Lebanese channel across the Arab world. The programme, which adopted a Western format, is a singing contest, where nominees from across the Arab world are admitted to represent their countries. During the mourning period following the assassination of the Lebanese Prime Minister Hariri, the programme took a political stance. The show aired after the assassination reflected the Lebanese public's mourning mood: contestants were dressed in black from head to toe (Kraidy 2007), as a sign of support for Lebanon and the Lebanese people. The nationalistic songs seemed to have an effect on the Arab public. As a result of this campaign, the Syrian contestant was voted out, as some Lebanese allegedly believed that the Syrian secret services were behind the assassination. This is another example of how the Arab media has successfully rallied public opinion, which led, in this case, to the action of voting the Syrian contestant out.

It is worth mentioning that *Star Academy* has been at the centre of debate in the national and regional media. Most of the Arab media have debated the pros and cons of the programme, but the prevailing view is that the programme promotes values incompatible with Islamic religion and culture. Nowhere has the debate been more heated than in Kuwait, where Islamists strongly opposed the broadcast of the programme, but what triggered the debate and protest was the ministry of information's decision to allow a concert by the contestants of *Star Academy* to be held in Kuwait (Kaidy 2007). As a result of this protest, the Kuwaiti minister of information resigned from his post. This is an example of how the Arab public's action can lead at times to changes, though small in their nature. *Star Academy* is but one example of the programmes that have sparked heated debate and engaged the Arab public in discussing political matters. *Star Academy*, in this case, is 'explored as a political space, using the Lebanese–Syrian conflict in the wake of the assassination of Rafiq al-Hariri' (Kraidy 2007: 45).

The programme could also be used as an example to demonstrate the impact of the transnational media on the Arab public sphere. Here, the Arab public, especially the young generation, voice their opinions and make their choices and preferences clear by voting contestants in and out. This conforms with Hahn's statement that 'public spheres are considered as intermediate spaces between governmental structures and society. Communication is not limited to taking place only within different national public spheres but can be transnational' (Hahn 2007: 18).

Today, Arab transnational communication faces many challenges, some of which come from the West. The control of the flow of information by Western media and organisations has dictated the pattern and pace of that flow. Many Arab media have found themselves obliged to adopt a foreign cultural media model (McQuail 1994: 113). The Arab media has realised that the threat the global media poses is authentic and real, and if it does not act swiftly it will lose some of its Arab market shares to this newly developed media. Therefore, it faces two major options. The first is to accept the status quo, by ignoring the global development of technology and the newly developed means of information, and so risk losing its core audience to the international media. The second option is to modernise and compete with the international media in order to retain its core audience. Although most of the Arab state-run media would accept the first option, the transnational Arab media have taken the global threat seriously and opted for the second choice. It has adopted high-tech means of circulating information, and has followed Western media models. This new strategy has far-reaching effects on both the Arab public and the development of the Arab media. The Arab public, as has been discussed earlier, has become more interactive and respondent to the major issues facing the Arab world.

Despite its efforts to generate news information from the Arab world, most of the Arab media still relies on foreign media agencies for news and information (Glass 2001). This has an impact on the nature and genre of information presented to Arab audiences. The outcome of this is that the Arab consumer has become well informed about issues related to Europe and the United States, but their knowledge of the South is very limited. The prevalence of information coming from the West could be explained by the fact that domestic news agencies have taken a back seat when it comes to the circulation of information about the South. However, the launch of Al-Jazeera English has changed this by focusing on the South in its broadcasting.

The Arab media and national political systems

Rugh (2007) asserted that in order to understand the Arab media, we need to understand the national political system of the country in which that media is operating. To explain his hypothesis that the Arab media is influenced by national political structures, Rugh categorises it into three sub-categories. The first is what he calls the 'mobilisation' media system. This system is exploited by the national government and regimes to mobilise their public to support them, using the media as a weapon or tool to promote government policies. Some of these media belong to private sectors, but the government has total control over its editorial practices (Rugh 2007). In order to avoid criticism over their own-ership of the media, some governments have allowed private media to operate under tight control and within strict rules. The second category is the 'loyal' media. This type of media, Rugh postulates, exists in countries where there are no political rival parties and no opposition. The government seems to adopt a passive role vis-à-vis the media, but its coverage and broadcast are a testimony that this type of media adheres to government rules and broadcasting norms. The 'loyalist' media passively accepts the status quo and operates within the strict rules laid down by the government. Its survival is based on its daily service to the government. The third category is what Rugh calls the 'diverse' media system. This type of media reflects the diversity of opinions and political parties and because of the differences in opinions, it tends to operate relatively freely. There are restrictions on the way this type of media operates, but they 'are relatively minimal or not strictly enforced' (Rugh 2007: 2). Rugh realises that his categories do not encompass all Arab countries, and therefore adds another category called the 'transitional' media system. This includes the media operating in countries when a transition in the political system is occurring, or is envisaged to occur in the short term. The outcome of this transition in the political system usually has an impact on the operation of the media.

Rugh's categorisation is valid when considering the Arab press, but raises here the question of where to fit in the transnational media. Although some of this media might fit well within the category of 'diverse' media, others, as in the case of Al-Jazeera and BBC Arabic, might not fit within this category, partly because they seem to operate more independently and freely.

Al-Arabiya and the public sphere

At the beginning of this chapter we discussed the impact on the Arab public of Al-Jazeera as a transnational Arab broadcaster. We have come to the conclusion that the proliferation of transnational media has created an atmosphere of competition between Al-Jazeera and its other rivals, especially Al-Arabiya. This section will help us to understand the role of Al-Arabiya, as a new broadcaster, in engaging with the Arab public. Al-Saggaf (2006) conducted a study of Al-Arabiya's website. His analysis reveals that the site is a public place where different Arab readers have access to a wide range of materials, on which they comment and express their opinions and views. His findings are very revealing; they indicate that Al-Arabiya's online material provides a platform for readers to debate, discuss and voice their opinions on issues of importance to them. Al-Saggaf noted that comments posted on the channel's site reflect a diverse range of opinions, and that the site nurtured public debate among readers. He also concluded that some of what has been published is intended to serve the Saudi government, the sponsor of the channel.

Al-Arabiya is just one example of the transnational Arab media that have opened their programmes and websites to viewers and readers to express their own opinions on published materials. Similarly, Al-Jazeera offered its readers the opportunity to express their opinions on materials published on its website. This phenomenon of encouraging the Arab reader to contribute to the discussion, and to evaluate and assess published materials, could be compared to the traditional meeting rooms where Arab intellectuals used to meet to discuss intellectual issues. The only difference is that the online public sphere can draw readers from across the Arab world, with different political orientations and individual opinions. As the new Arab media started cementing its power and existence in the Arab world, the new Arab public has found newly developed means of sharing information and debating contentious issues. It should be said here that the Arab media has not only contributed to disseminating a wide range of news and information, but has created an online public sphere where people can voice their opinions.

The discourse of globalisation and the Arab media

As alluded to earlier in this chapter, the term globalisation is often the subject of fierce debate among those who embrace the term and those who reject it. Since the 1970s, the pros and cons of the term have been the subject of extensive debate among scholars. Some consider globalisation a threatening influence on the system of democratisation, and to have some negative impact on workers' rights; they have also stated that globalisation can weaken the authority and limit the power of individual states (Martin and Schumann 1997). Others see a global benefit in the flow of international trade and the global economy (Levitt 1983; Ohmae 1990). Another group have expressed their scepticism over the effects of globalisation (Fiss and Mirsch 2005). Globalisation has become a notion attached to modernity and has been regarded as the 'umbrella construct' which brings different cultures and groups to coexist. The question here is: how does globalisation affect the operation of the Arab media and its discourse?

Most of the transnational Arab media has realised that, in order to attract viewers, it should provide an alternative approach to the existing state channel models. This means that the new Arab channels have to modernise their broadcasting approach, including their discursive practices. What goes unnoticed in almost all transnational Arab channels is the prevalence of a discourse of liberalism and accountability, where both citizens and governments are allowed to contribute to debates and discussions concerning issues of importance to them. Globalisation has not only affected the content aired on these channels, but has also changed the future vision of most of the Arab media. Transnational channels are no longer, for instance, constrained to safeguarding Arab culture and religion. This is evident in the wide range of programmes that are open to debating issues related to Islamic jurisprudence, women, governance and other former taboos. The modern Arab media has started adopting a new secularist discourse, but more importantly an inclusive discourse which incorporates both governments and citizens. Fiss and Mirsch (2005: 34) noted that the more the discourse of globalisation diffuses across discursive fields, 'the greater [the] heterogeneity of discourse communities', and this could generate a variety of opinions; however, the question that could be posed here is: how does globalisation affect the discourse of citizenship and media in the Arab world?

The argument around citizenship and globalisation centres on the impact of globalisation on the power status of the citizen. This means that some citizens might feel they have no power and influence over their political leaders because of different global factors (Poster 2001). The tide of the global market means that citizens are no longer in control of their own economy, or the flow of the labour that follows it. The other concern for citizens is the threat to their culture. In the Arab world, the media is constantly blamed for promoting other cultures and mobilising the Arab public against its own governments. The role of the transnational Arab media in bringing the Arab public together and in promoting shared values has been seen by some as an attempt to revive the notion of Arab nationalism.

Is the Arab media a global phenomenon?

Before embarking on answering this question, I would like to divide the Arab media into state-owned media and transnational media to ensure clear discussion and debate about what is and what is not global.

As its name suggests, the state-owned media is run and administered by the state. It is limited to the geographical borders of that state, and therefore directed towards the local citizens. It could be described as local media because it deals with domestic issues concerning local citizens. It is often, as mentioned earlier, used for propaganda to promote governments' policies. This type of media has no strategic aims of having regional or international influence (Kirchner 2001: 137).

The second type is the transnational Arab media, which aims at disseminating its information beyond the geographical boundaries of individual Arab states. Al-Jazeera, Al-Arabiya and Al-Hurra could be cited as examples of transnational regional media. It is considered regional because of the accessibility of this media across the Arab world. Its reach is mostly confined to the Arab public; however, Al-Jazeera can be considered a global channel because of its ability to convey its message in both Arabic and English. The Arabic channel disseminates news and information across the Arab world and in the Arab diaspora, while its English sister broadcasts to the English-speaking world. So, Al-Jazeera here manages to 'transcend nation-state boundaries and language communities' (Barker 2000). Based on Barker's definition of global media, Al-Jazeera could be categorised as a global channel. According to Saghieh (2004), Al-Jazeera's impact stems from its ability to use a high-tech approach, or what he referred to as 'capitalist globalisation', and its successful outreach to 'ethnic and religious populism'. Unlike Barker, Saghieh examined the existing features that could characterise Al-Jazeera as a global phenomenon.

Conclusion

Over the course of this chapter, I have argued that the advent of the global media has led to the development of the Arab media. The Arab media in turn has moved quite swiftly to counter the hegemony of the international media, providing platforms for the Arab public to express their opinions and debate issues close to their hearts. The satellite Arab media has created a culture of debate and discussion in the Arab world, where different views are appreciated and respected. Although some of the state-run media do still follow the traditional broadcasting system, the new transnational media have adopted a global outlook, breaking all borders, barriers and taboos. Al-Jazeera, Al-Arabiya and other transnational channels have demonstrated the ability not only to provide reliable coverage, but to motivate the Arab public to take part in that coverage. The analysis in this chapter has also shown quite clearly that the global operation of the media has opened the Arab media market to competition, and this has had some very positive effects on the development of the Arab media which have been reflected not only in the open way in which the new Arab media has conducted itself, but also in its attempt to win over the Arab public. The fierce competition between channels such as Al-Jazeera, Al-Hurra and Al-Arabiya, the subject of study of the next chapter, has created a media practice based on openness and transparency. The following chapter sheds more light on these three channels and their quest to win over the hearts and minds of the Arab public.

Chapter 3

Al-Jazeera, Al-Hurra and Al-Arabiya: Different Channels or Three Sides of the Same Triangle?

Al-Jazeera

Al-Jazeera and objectivity

Most of the Western media pride themselves on the fact that they provide impartial, fair and free coverage of news. Objectivity is at the heart of Western media practices and it is a concept which goes hand in hand with the right to freedom of expression and the right to communicate. Objectivity is a concept that was lacking in some Arab media because of their unfailing support for governments; however, the launch of Al-Jazeera has changed this and the channel considers objectivity part and parcel of its broadcasting practices. This is clearly articulated in the channel's motto, 'The Opinion and the Other Opinion' (El-Nawawy 2006: 29). Al-Jazeera's new approach and commitment to freedom of expression and representation of all views is a new phenomenon to hit the Arab world. It has been welcomed by the Arab public and media observers alike. According to El-Nawawy (2006: 30), Al-Jazeera believes that 'public discourse can only be equitable and effective if all possible opinions and views are expressed and demonstrated equally, whether they are Israeli, Palestinian, American or Turkish.' It appears from this that Al-Jazeera has adopted a pluralistic approach where all individuals, governments and organisations are treated equally and fairly in the channel's coverage.

Al-Jazeera was the first Arabic channel to welcome Israeli officials on its programmes to discuss the Arab–Israeli conflict. It is also the channel that provided platforms for American officials to explain their foreign policy and their presence in Iraq to the Arab public. Although Al-Jazeera has tried to open its programmes to Western officials, however, the channel covers the news from an Arab perspective 'to correct anti-Arab distortions and to counter dominant Western perspective like CNN and the BBC' (El-Nawawy 2006: 30). Mohammed Jasim al-Ali, the former Al-Jazeera managing director, put it this way: 'they [Al-Jazeera staff] take the professional experience from the BBC, but their background as Arabs means we can adapt this experience and apply it to the Arab world. We know the mentality of the Arabs' (El-Nawawy and Iskandar 2002: 54). Interestingly enough, al-Ali's view could be considered as biased towards the Arab public, and some might regard it as an attempt to give up objectivity in order to gain popularity among the Arab public. Zayani (2005) considers the launch of Al-Jazeera an end to what he describes 'as a one-size-fits-all media'. Al-Jazeera's monopoly over the coverage of the war on Afghanistan ended an era of complete control by the Western media over the dissemination of news and information. According to Zayani (2005: 32), 'Al-Jazeera prides itself on reporting Arab news from the Arab world better than other international stations, which makes it appealing to the Arab-Muslim world.'

Some Western scholars and observers have hailed Al-Jazeera as a herald of democratisation. Abunimah and Ibish (2001) state: 'Al-Jazeera presents the best trends of openness and democratization in the Arab world. It is a long-overdue two-way street in the global flow of information and opinion. It should be celebrated and encouraged.'

The arrival of Al-Jazeera has generated a heated debate as to whether an Arabic channel operating from the Middle East can rise to prominence and rival some of the finest well-established channels such as the BBC and CNN. Although this is a legitimate question to ask, the main question that occupied everyone's minds was whether the channel could change the Arab media landscape.

It is fair to say that, despite its pitfalls, Al-Jazeera has managed to dictate the pace and format of broadcasting in the Middle East. It has contributed to creating a culture of debate and discussion, where passiveness has been replaced by activeness. These changes are not only reflected in the sheer numbers of people who express their opinions through call-in programmes, but are manifested in the willingness of journalists and the elite to contribute to the discussion using Al-Jazeera's platforms (Zayani 2005).

As for Al-Jazeera's approach to dealing with information, some observers consider the channel to lack the necessary analytical skills in dealing with complex issues and feel its broadcasting is often exaggerated (Zayani 2005). The channel operates around the clock and news is fed in as it develops. This, according to Zayani (2005), leaves Arab viewers with a lot of information to digest in a very limited timescale.

Al-Jazeera and the West

As Al-Jazeera started its broadcasting, Western governments queued up to express their satisfaction and shower the channel with praise, while some Arab governments expressed their discontent with the direction and approach of Al-Jazeera. Impressed by its coverage, the US government considers the channel unique, while *Harvard International Review* regards the channel as a pioneering network and Thomas Friedman, *New York Times* columnist, 'hailed it as a beacon of freedom and the biggest media phenomenon to hit the Arab world' (Zayani 2005: 21).

September 11th was a turning point for the channel. Being the only channel allowed access to the Taliban-controlled Afghanistan, Al-Jazeera, similar to CNN during the Gulf War in 1991, was the only one to report the war from within Afghanistan. Its colourful logo featured worldwide. Unheard of previously outside the Middle East and North Africa, Al-Jazeera now became a worldwide celebrity. The channel dominated the dissemination of information, at least for a while, until the Taliban were kicked out of the country. The war on Afghanistan was considered a 'landmark in the network's history, rendering it almost overnight a household name in the West' Karaiskou (2007: 3). Although Al-Jazeera enjoyed the monopoly over the dissemination of news, the tide turned against the channel, and its coverage was heavily criticised by the Western governments and media. Its coverage of unfiltered graphic images of Afghan civilians and its airing of Bin Laden's messages angered the US government, and led to heightened tension between the channel and other Western governments. Al-Jazeera became part of the news it covers. It has been accused of being the mouthpiece of Bin Laden; however, this did not deter the channel from airing live images of affected civilians. In the last days of the war, Al-Jazeera's bureau in Kabul was struck by a US missile. The US military denied Al-Jazeera's accusation that US forces directly targeted its bureau, insisting that it was struck inadvertently. Al-Jazeera was then the focus of criticism from the Western media and Western governments alike. The tension between the channel and the US government reached its peak when a top-secret British government memo was leaked, containing information about George Bush's suggestion of bombing Al-Jazeera's headquarters in Qatar. Despite the tension between the channel and Western governments, high-ranking officials, such as Condoleezza Rice, Tony Blair, Colin Powell and others, continued to be interviewed by Al-Jazeera (Karaiskou 2007). Al-Jazeera's airing of Bin Laden's messages 'changed the Western perception of [the network] from a "phenomenon of democracy" to a "mouthpiece of Bin Laden" – although Al-Jazeera perceives itself as nothing more than a delivery system in a competitive media environment' (Bessaiso 2005: 153). Al-Jazeera consistently argued that airing Bin Laden's tapes offered the Arab audience the opportunity to hear the other side of the story (Bessaiso 2005).

In his comparison between CNN and Al-Jazeera of the coverage of the war on Afghanistan, El-Nawawy (2006) argued that, while CNN focused on the technological advances of the weaponry, Al-Jazeera took a completely different approach by focusing on the 'collateral damage' that was caused by the US bombing of buildings, mosques, villages and infrastructure (El-Nawawy 2006: 38). For El-Nawawy, Al-Jazeera humanised the personal suffering of the Afghan people. It is this feeling of being on the side of the innocent people that made Al-Jazeera popular among Arab viewers, and give it a sense of legitimacy and credibility among the Arab public.

Al-Jazeera followed the same approach in its coverage of the war on Iraq. Prior to the war, Al-Jazeera covered the anti-war demonstrations and anti-American feelings in the region. Again, during the war, Al-Jazeera focused on the humanitarian crisis it generated. This included Iraqi civilian deaths and the public unrest which characterised the whole of Iraq, and which manifested in the looting of governmental as well as private institutions. In its coverage, 'Al-Jazeera fed a strong desire in the Arab world to support Iraqi civilians, who represented the "underdog"' (El-Nawawy 2006: 40). By focusing on human suffering and tragedy, Al-Jazeera appealed to Arab public sentiment. This has attracted sharp criticism of the channel. Some dismiss 'the channel as tabloid journalism' (Zayani 2005: 22), while others point out its pitfalls:

> its reporters are sometimes guilty of over-exuberance. For example, they are inclined to claim that one telegenic student demonstration is representative of a whole country's 'street opinion.' Even Al-Jazeera's supporters say that its success with audiences has caused a strident and highly politicized tone to creep into some of its programming. (*The Economist* 2001, in Zayani 2005: 22)

Thomas Friedman, who previously hailed Al-Jazeera a beacon of freedom, turned against the channel because 'it goes over the edge and burns people unfairly because some of its broadcasters have their own agendas, and sometimes it hypes the fighting in the West Bank in inflammatory ways' (Friedman 2001).

Al-Jazeera has also been criticised for its coverage of the on-going Palestinian–Israeli conflict. The channel's coverage of the second intifada has extended its reach in the Arab world and made it popular among the Arab public. The Palestinian cause is close to the Arab public's hearts, and is one that they identify with quite easily. Al-Jazeera has played a leading role in bringing to the fore the Palestinian plight and suffering. The coverage of live demonstrations of Palestinians against the occupation has helped to mobilise the Arab public to help and support the Palestinians and their intifada (Zayani 2005). Zayani (2005: 173) argues that Al-Jazeera capitalised on the Palestinian cause by covering the intifada in detail, 'airing raw footage and images of incursions, death and demolition in the West Bank and the Gaza Strip rarely displayed by western media'. This coverage has rallied the Arab public and significantly shaped their opinions about what is happening in Palestine. As a result, the Arab public took to the street to demonstrate in support of Palestinians. The death of a twelve-year-old boy, Mohamed Al-Durra, in the arms of his father, caused by Israeli soldiers, fuelled feelings of anger among the Arab public. The death of Mohamed Al-Durra became a rallying point for the Palestinian cause (Zayani 2005: 173). It has strengthened the Palestinian resolve to fight the occupation, and it has also cemented the existing relationship between the Palestinians and the Arab public. The role of Al-Jazeera in this cannot be underestimated.

The coverage of the second intifada differs remarkably between the Arab and the Western media. While the Arab media aired footage of the Israeli army incursion into Gaza, the Western media found it extremely difficult to refer to the occupation as 'illegal' (Sakr 2001). It could be argued that the second intifada has instilled confidence in the Arab media, especially Al-Jazeera, which, among other Arab broadcasters, has captured 'the carnage in the Occupied Territories, which was made all the more horrific by the number of Palestinian children killed and injured by bullets to the head or upper body' (Sakr 2001: 192). These scenes, aired live on Al-Jazeera, showing young Palestinians throwing stones at the Israeli army, had 'a galvanizing effect on young people throughout the Arab world' (Sakr 2001: 192).

Al-Jazeera's programmes

Around-the-clock news is Al-Jazeera's major focus. The news bulletins are extended reports gathered from across the globe by its reporters, who are scattered across the world in twenty-six countries. The channel also has other scheduled programmes in which it covers national and international issues. It offers a wide range of programmes in which political, cultural, historical and religious topics are discussed and debated. Each programme has its own format and presenter. Some of these programmes are more popular than others, but all seem to contribute to the channel's chief aim of offering a platform for voiceless people.

One programme, *Bi La Hudud* (*Without Limits*) discusses medical and cultural issues. Another, *al-Itijah al-Mu'akis* (*The Opposite Direction*), presented by Faisal Al-Qasim, is the most controversial programme and is widely viewed across the Arab world. It has been noted for its 'daring handling of local and pan-Arab issues, and according to its host, for breaking significant social, political, and cultural taboos' (Ayish 2005: 111). It hosts guests from across the political spectrum, including dissenting Arab voices. The discussion is often fierce and heated, with viewers contributing to the discussion through call-in shows, some of which have changed Arab culture and encouraged debate and discussion among people of different views. The most discussed themes are 'inter-Arab conflicts, Arab conflicts with the international community, [. . .] terrorism and political scandals' (Bahry 2001: 92). The idea of calling in and contributing to the programme is exciting, and most Arab viewers appear to enjoy expressing their views on air. The presenter, Faisal Al-Qasim, does not shy away from siding with guests to ignite debate. According to Al-Qasim, this type of discussion contributes immensely to the wider social debate that is absent from schools, institutions and homes. He says:

> Dialogue is something missing among the Arabs. It is missing in schools, as much as it is missing everywhere else in the life of the Arabs. At home, the father is a dictator. At work, the employer is a dictator, and in the life of the Arab countries, the political leader is a dictator. Through programs such as mine, we hope to implement new rules, those that educate the Arab human being to listen, not only to his own opinion, but to that of the other side as well. The debate-based media must enter into force and strongly in the political life of the Arabs, whether the Arab regimes like it or not. (Bahry 2001: 93)

Al-Qasim's statement is a representation of Arab society that we rarely see exemplified in the Arab media's coverage. Encouraging debate and discussion live on Arab channels will not only empower the upcoming generation to speak their minds and express their opinions, but will also play down the power exercised in schools and workplaces.

Providing a platform for discussion and interaction grants the

Arab public a great opportunity to make their voices heard and 'their presence felt in a mediated context by transcending the special barriers which usually characterize the producer–audience relationship' (Coleman and Ross 2010: 53). Historically, the producer–audience relationship was felt in the audience's feedback to the editor about the content published in a newspaper or aired on radio and television. Before the advent of technology and online interactive processes, the British media was keen on receiving feedback through the concept of 'letters to the editor', which was designed to encourage the audience to provide feedback and comments on aspects of published content (Coleman and Ross 2010). Such a practice has helped in developing a variety of means of providing feedback. The online commentary spaces provided by channels have contributed to receiving prompt feedback and comments on online-published material. Arab readers have used the online means for providing feedback quite effectively. On Al-Jazeera's and Al-Arabiya's websites, for instance, different views are expressed on the published material. Readers have the opportunity not only to comment, but also to assess and evaluate the published material.

Arabic programmes such as *al-Itijah al-Mu'akis* (*The Opposite Direction*) do not only polarise opinions, but have at times caused strained relations between some other Arab countries and Qatar. Many Arab countries have expressed their discontent with the programme's coverage, and have complained directly to the Qatari government. Others have gone further and closed Al-Jazeera's bureaus in their country; Jordan, for instance, closed Al-Jazeera's bureau from November 1998 to February 1999 (Bahry 2001). Tunisia and Libya have gone even further and recalled their ambassadors in protest at Al-Jazeera giving a platform to their opposition. In March 2011 the Libyan regime arrested Al-Jazeera's Arabic team in Tripoli, accusing them of bias against the government. The Qatari government has maintained a consistent official response to these complaints, stating that Al-Jazeera is an independent channel and not a state-run channel. Whether this response is to be believed is a subject for another discussion. In some episodes of *The Opposite Direction*, the discussion has grown out of hand and the programme has turned into an arena for a bull fight.

Another programme which broke taboos is *Sharia and Life*, presented by Othman Othman. The programme discusses how

Islamic religion can be applied in modern societies. It also discusses themes including sexuality, circumcision of women and other sexual practices (Bahry 2001:93).

In addition to the above programmes, Al-Jazeera offers others that are designed to stimulate discussion and debate among the Arab public. For example, *More Than One Opinion* (*Akthar Min Rai*), aired from London and presented by the Lebanese-born Sami Haddad, invites different people from across the political spectrum to discuss current issues.

Al-Jazeera has also introduced programmes for women to debate issues related to them. Until now, the issue of women's roles and their status in Arab societies has often been sidelined in debates, but the launch of the weekly programme *Li Nissa Faqat* has given women a platform to discuss issues such as relationships between men and women, violence against women, family relationships, women at work, and women and leadership. The programme has provided women with a platform to express their views and voice their concerns.

The expansion of Al-Jazeera

A review of Al-Jazeera's achievements over the last fourteen years indicates that the channel has expanded beyond recognition, widening its programmes to reach out to a variety of Arab audiences through different sub-channels. The expansion of Al-Jazeera is considered part of the channel's vision of being a worldwide competitor. Waddah Khanfar, its managing director, set out this vision for the channel, saying:

> we are expanding globally because for us the competition is not Al Arabiya. They may have been set up to compete with us, but for the competition (and I say this in the collegial spirit of friendship and cooperation) it is the BBC World Service and CNN International because we see ourselves as a global broadcaster on the merits of our coverage and the fullness of our vision'. (qtd in Zayani and Sahraoui 2007: 163)

Capitalising on the popularity of the channel among the Arab public, Al-Jazeera launched its Arabic website in 2003 to interact with the Arab audience, followed by an English-language website designed for English speakers. Realising the importance of interacting with the Arab audience, the channel launched its mobile service in 2004. It has also established specialised channels like Al-Jazeera Sport, which covers all types of sporting activities across the globe, and a Children's Channel, which has an educational purpose.

As part of its outreach to non-Arabic speakers, Al-Jazeera has developed a multilingual website that can be accessed by speakers of French, Turkish and Urdu. This is part of the implementation of what the channel's managing director called a 'global vision'. The most important step towards the globalisation of Al-Jazeera was its launch of Al-Jazeera English in 2006. This is, as Zayani and Sahraoui (2007: 166) put it, was 'the first Arab media outlet to transmit news in English twenty-four hours a day for what is perceived as "a ready audience" '. The bulk of Al-Jazeera English's audience is in Asian countries such as Pakistan, Indonesia and Malaysia, where a large Muslim population lives.

Although Al-Jazeera has been criticised for its narrow broadcasting approach and for creating division and friction among Arab countries, it is fair to say that the channel has introduced a new broadcasting culture to the Arab world. The expansion of Al-Jazeera is clearly reflected in the wide range of programmes on offer, specialised channels, and its successful attempts to reach out to a global audience. The question here is: could Al-Jazeera compete with media giants such as CNN, the BBC, etc.? A cursory assessment of the current situation suggests that the channel has yet to establish itself as a global competitor. This has been impeded by the fact that so many international channels have been launched since 2003, all of which have a vision of being globally influential.

Al-Jazeera and coverage of the wars on Afghanistan and Iraq

Al-Jazeera rose to prominence during its coverage of the war on Afghanistan. The channel's popularity was no longer confined to the Arab world; its logo was aired across the world. This was a clear indication of Al-Jazeera's monopoly over the coverage of the war, which sparked a blaze of controversy. Al-Jazeera's monopoly over the distribution of information meant that most of the international media relied on the channel for their coverage; however, its coverage of the war on Afghanistan was not to the liking of the US administration. Many US officials have been vocal in their criticism of Al-Jazeera's practices. US Secretary of State Colin Powell said during an interview on ABC's *Good Morning America* that Al-Jazeera 'is an important station in the Arab world; our concern, however, is that they give an undue amount of time and attention to some very vitriolic, irresponsible kinds of statements' (El-Nawawy and Iskandar 2002: 176). The US officials' discontent with the channel was discussed on numerous occasions with Qatari diplomats and the government. On 3 October 2001, Colin Powell asked the Emir of Qatar to 'tone down' Al-Jazeera. The Emir of Qatar later confirmed at a press conference that Al-Jazeera was a subject of discussion during their meeting. He said that Qatar 'heard from this administration, as well as previous US administrations, on this issue. Parliamentary life requires you have free and credible media, and that is what we are trying to do' (El-Nawawy and Iskandar 2002: 176). The US officials' discontent with Al-Jazeera's coverage is in stark contrast to their policies of promoting freedom and democracy across the Arab world. This has been reiterated by Mohammed Jasim Al-Ali, Al-Jazeera's managing director, who said 'we learned media independence from the United States, and now the American officials want us to give up what we learned from them' (El-Nawawy and Iskandar 2002: 176). The US government's complaints intensified when Al-Jazeera started airing Bin Laden's messages, which the US administration considered to be a threat to its security because they believed these messages held coded signals to al-Qaeda operatives. Al-Jazeera, however, defended its airing of the messages, arguing that the messages represented the other side of the story, and that its audience would be interested in hearing both sides of the story.

Mohammed Jasim Al-Ali said 'our critics tend to forget that bin Laden is one side in this war that we need to present to our viewers. How would our news be balanced without presenting both sides?' (El-Nawawy and Iskandar 2002: 176). US officials' pressure on Al-Jazeera prompted the International Press Institute to write to Colin Powell, expressing their concerns over any attempt to curtail the news reporting of an independent channel, which could be considered as 'an infringement of editorial independence and has serious consequences for press freedom' (El-Nawawy and Iskandar 2002: 177). Al-Jazeera's insistence on presenting a balanced news story turned its old friends into enemies. The United States' frustration with the channel's coverage of the war on Afghanistan was evident in their open criticism of the channel, which they labelled a mouthpiece of Bin Laden. Being undeterred by such criticism, the channel continued to air live images of dead civilians. This has only severed relations between the channel and its old allies. The coverage of the war on Afghanistan continues to exasperate the US administration. US officials repeatedly accuse the channel of irresponsibility in its coverage of the war. The US administration's call to international media to refrain from airing Bin Laden's messages sparked a fierce debate between those who felt that his messages were a threat to the American people, and those who considered that airing his messages was part and parcel of responsible journalism and a vital aspect of freedom of expression. The then National Security Advisor, Condoleezza Rice, strongly objected to the airing of Bin Laden's messages on the grounds that they contained coded messages for sleeper cells in the United States. Although some media leaders such as Rupert Murdoch took Rice's claim seriously and promised to act in line with her message, others were sceptical about the US government's move. They dismissed the idea that al-Qaeda sleeper cells would use Bin Laden's messages to plot terrorist attacks against the United States. Gerard Baker, a London *Times* columnist, rejected the idea that al-Qaeda associates were waiting for signals from their leader to carry out attacks on US soil. The White House's calls for a ban on broadcasting Bin Laden's speeches came under fire from Reporters sans frontières, who considered the White House's move as a 'censorship' (El-Nawawy and Iskandar 2002: 179).

Although US government had military superiority over the Taliban, the information war was one of their concerns. They felt that the monopoly of Al-Jazeera over the distribution of information in the Arab world, and its popularity among the Arab public, would have some negative impact on the United States's image in the Arab and Muslim worlds. An American official is reported to have said, 'We are getting hammered in the Arab world' (El-Nawawy and Iskandar 2002: 189). The fear of losing the information war prompted the US government to take drastic measures to refine its image in the Arab world. The immediate first step taken by the government was to launch its own Arabic channel that would promote US policies directly to the Arab public. Al-Hurra and Radio Sawa were launched for this purpose. Many analysts were of the view, however, that to win public diplomacy, one must take bold action. Osama Siblani, publisher of *Arab American News* in Dearborn, Michigan, clearly stated that 'you cannot win with words; you have to win with actions' (El-Nawawy and Iskandar 2002: 191). This action, he pointed out, includes resolving the long-standing Palestinian–Israeli conflict.

Al-Jazeera and the Arab audience

Since the launch of Al-Jazeera, many media observers have been eager to see the impact of the channel on the Arab public. Although it is quite challenging to measure this impact, many incidents following its broadcasts have been linked to Al-Jazeera's coverage of national and regional events. Critics of Al-Jazeera blamed the demonstrations which swept the Arab world after the eruption of the second intifada on the channel's live coverage of the clash between Palestinians and the Israeli military. These demonstrations were seen to be sparked by Al-Jazeera's coverage of the conflict; however, many observers expressed their doubts about the channel's ability to mobilise the Arab public to rally behind any Arab cause. The same level of protests erupted in 1998 when the channel covered the American–British bombing of Iraq.

Al-Jazeera's political talk shows have revolutionised the Arab public's political thinking and behaviour (Lynch 2006). The Arab public has become more critical, active and aware of the main issues surrounding it; however, the lack of action and real change, which is generally due to a lack of organisation, has generated a level of frustration and disillusionment among the Arab public (Lynch 2006). The new media have become the only means through which they channel their views and thoughts but this is still insufficient as the majority of the Arab public do not have access to these means of communication. The danger is that the frustration of the Arab public and their discontent with the status quo could be exploited by extreme forces who promote confrontation and violent means, rather than debate. The direction which this public mood will take is yet to be known, but what has become apparent is that it has broken the barrier of fear that has long gripped its movement and action; however, this change cannot come about without proper structure, organisation and leadership.

The new Arab media have contributed immensely to changing the Arab public's opinions and attitudes towards politics. The Iraq issue has brought home to the Arab public the question of Arab identity and, similarly to the Palestinian issue, it has become the unifying factor among the Arab public. Lynch (2006: 11) summarised this quite clearly, saying the 'suffering Iraqi people became a vital touchstone for all Arab debate, a starting point of consensus rather than a point to be established' (Lynch 2006: 11). It could be argued here that Al-Jazeera has played a crucial role in persuading the Arab public to rally in support of their fellow Iraqis.

As mentioned earlier, Al-Jazeera's coverage of conflicts in the Middle East from an Arab perspective has increased its popularity and viewership across the Arab world. For instance, during its coverage of the conflict in Lebanon, as the statistics in Table 3.1 demonstrate, Al-Jazeera's viewership increased quite substantially.

The statistics show that Al-Jazeera enjoys a good spread of viewership across the Arab world. The presence of the channel in almost all Arab countries has meant that it can have a great influence on the Arab public. This influence could culminate in creating a homogeneous audience who have become aware of what is going around them, not only within their own country, but across the region. It could be also argued here that the new Arab transnational channels have contributed to creating a new audience that has started acting on issues beyond their individual countries. Despite the sharp criticism directed towards Al-Jazeera, the channel should be credited for its ability to create a new Arab public. The public has matured over the last few years or so. It has become more aware of the issues surrounding it, and as a result it has started voicing its concerns collectively under the leadership of a seemingly young, fearless generation that has high aspirations.

One would envisage that, given the current changes that are sweeping the Arab world, in the coming years we will see the Arab public grow in both confidence and organisation.

Table 3.1 *Al-Jazeera's total potential audience. (Source: adapted from Al-Jazeera Television. Viewers Demographics, Alexandria, VA: Allied Media Corp., available online at http://www.allied-media.com/aljazeera/ al_jazeera_viewers_demographics.html)*

Country/ region	Total population	Arabs (%)	Total adult Arabs (15 years +)	Potential audience
Algeria	32,818,500	99.0	21,833,492	5,240,038
Bahrain	667,238	73.0	346,804	151,553
Cyprus	771,657	3.2	19,285	4,821
Egypt	74,718,797	94.0	46,425,777	4,642,578
Europe	n/a	n/a	n/a	4,000,000
Iran	68,278,826	1.0	482,731	289,639
Iraq	24,683,313	75.0	10,977,903	5,159,615
Israel	6,116,533	19.9	889,766	418,190
Jordan	5,460,265	98.0	3,430,029	1,783,615
Kuwait	2,183,161	80.0	1,259,247	871,021
Lebanon	3,727,703	95.0	2,581,621	1,530,901
Libya	5,499,074	97.0	3,493,837	1,921,610
Morocco	31,689,265	99.1	20,977,913	8,223,342
Oman	2,807,125	75.0	1,216,889	717,964
Qatar	817,052	40.0	246,096	170,102
Saudi Arabia	24,293,844	90.0	12,615,793	6,463,071
Syria	17,585,540	90.3	9,750,162	3,705,062
Tunisia	9,924,742	98.0	7,100,160	1,633,037
Turkey	68,109,469	10.0	4,958,369	495,837
United Arab Emirates	2,484,818	40.0	728,549	378,845
United States	n/a	n/a	n/a	1,000,000
West Bank and Gaza Strip	3,512,062	88.6	1,680,311	1,663,508
Yemen	19,349,881	98.0	10,088,254	2,723,829
Grand total	**405,498,865**	–	**161,102,989**	**53,208,177**

Al-Hurra and Radio Sawa

The date 11 September 2001 marked a turning point for both the Arab media and the US international media. As mentioned earlier, the unpopularity of US public diplomacy in the Arab world, especially after the war on Afghanistan, urged the Bush, Jr. administration to review its channels of communication with the Arab and Muslim worlds. Prior to the events of September 11th, Voice of America Arabic was active in promoting the United States's policies in the region; however, its remit was very limited and it could not compete with new Arab media channels such as Al-Jazeera. Bush's administration, then, decided to launch an Arabic channel that would rival Al-Jazeera and promote freedom and democracy in the region. In addition to the channel, Radio Sawa was also launched to target Arab youth by offering a mixture of Western and Arabic music. It should be said here that both Al-Hurra and Radio Sawa have different aims and objectives, although they both work towards improving and refining US policy in the region. Radio Sawa's main aims and objectives are completely different from those of Voice of America Arabic (VOA).

VOA's aim was to represent American values and institutions by delivering accurate and objective news about American policies in the Middle East. Although its charter does not explicitly refer to the promotion of freedom and democracy, VOA's broadcasting messages were tacitly geared towards that aim. VOA's sole aim was to introduce the Arab public to the American culture, policies and institutions. After September 11th, however, the US government reviewed its approach 'of communicating with the Arab public' (Lahlali 2009). In 2004, President Bush laid the blame on Arab channels for spreading 'hateful propaganda' against the United States. To combat these feelings of anti-Americanism, the United States launched Radio Sawa and Al-Hurra, which have been regarded as a new model within US international broadcasting (Pattiz 2004). More than $200 million has been invested in these two Arabic sources. Radio Sawa is solely directed at the Arab youth generation. Its programmes comprise 75 per cent pop music and Western songs, along with Arabic songs. This shift in policy in focusing on the Arab youth generation came after nineteen young Saudis were involved in the attack on the United States on September 11th. Although both radio stations have different aims and objectives, both have been set up to combat anti-American feelings and to promote American public diplomacy during and after the war.

The launch of VOA occurred in 1942 during the Second World War. It transmitted war news to the Arab world and part of its broadcasting was intended to explain American policies during the war. As the war came to an end, VOA terminated its service but it was revived during the Cold War. In 1950, VOA was on air for half an hour a day, but later on the service gathered momentum and started broadcasting English lessons. As the Swiss crisis grew deeper and deeper in 1956, VOA's air time surged to fourteen hours a day, only to be reduced to eight hours a day in 1958. The Second World War, the Cold War and the Swiss crisis are good examples of how VOA was used in wartime to promote and explain to the Arab public the United States's political stance. The same could be said of Al-Hurra and Radio Sawa, which were launched to explain the US government's policies after the war on Iraq.

Referring to the charter mentioned above, it could be said that the aims of VOA were very broad. Despite its popularity in the Arab world, VOA has gone through difficult broadcasting stages, especially during the Gulf War, which involved the United States against an Arab country for the first time in history. VOA had to show transparency and impartiality in its broadcasting. After the Gulf War, the American government stopped investing any further in VOA's programmes, which has had a knock-on-effect on the station's performance.

After 9/11, the US government realised the importance of maintaining a proper channel of communication with the Arab public, rivalling other channels that are seen to broadcast anti-American feelings. This led to the launch of Radio Sawa and Al-Hurra, with completely different objectives. Al-Hurra was launched on 14 February 2004 as a 24-hour, Arabic-language, satellite television network. Before the establishment of Radio Sawa and Al-Hurra, American media policy was to project a good image of the United States to the Arab world, especially the Arab political elite. This has become impossible with the emergence of new Arab media outlets such as Al-Jazeera, which have insisted on showing both faces of the coin. The US government's frustration with Al-Jazeera, coupled with the unsatisfactory performance of VOA, led the government to think of a new broadcasting alternative to rival Al-Jazeera and reach out to the Arab youth generation. The aims and objectives of the new radio station and television channel were thought through, and the US government decided that at the heart of the American image are freedom and democracy, which should be promoted to the Arab world. The government was of the opinion that the spread of freedom and democracy would allow the Arab people to avenge their anger and frustration on their governments, and not on the United States. This encouraged the US government to scrap VOA and replace it with Radio Sawa and Al-Hurra. Radio Sawa was directed to the Arab youth generation and was set to provide entertainment and brief news at the stroke of each hour. The first-year investment in Radio Sawa was $35 million, and in Al-Hurra it was $102 million, making the $4.5 million invested in VOA look like a drop in the ocean in comparison. Although many critics felt that the newly established channel and radio were not making any difference on the ground, the Broadcasting Board of Governors (BBG) justified their move by the fact that the new demographic changes in the Middle East, where half of the population are under the age of thirty-five, requires new broadcasting strategies to win the hearts and minds of the Arab youth generation. One way of achieving this is through winning their ears by broadcasting a wide range of Western and Arabic pop music. The replacement of VOA with Radio Sawa and Al-Hurra angered VOA employees, who expressed their discontent through a petition, accusing the management of 'dismantling' a radio service and replacing it with a music station. Recent statistics show that Radio Sawa is popular in countries like Bahrain, Jordan, Kuwait, Morocco, Qatar, Syria and the UAE, with Qatar registering the highest audience, with 75 per cent of adults aged between fifteen and twenty-nine years listening to Sawa, as demonstrated by the statistics in Figure 3.1.

Unlike VOA Arabic, whose identity was known to its listeners, Radio Sawa's identity and whereabouts remain hidden away from its listeners. Most Arab listeners have no idea that the pop song-

generous radio is American sponsored. The question here is: why has Radio Sawa's identity been kept secret from its listeners? The US government has realised that its image has been tarnished in the Middle East because of the wars on Iraq and Afghanistan. There was a growing fear that revealing the identity of Radio Sawa might lead to a boycott of the station by young Arab listeners, who are sceptical of American policies in the Middle East.

Figure 3.1 *Radio Sawa listeners.*
(Source: Broadcasting Board of Governors)

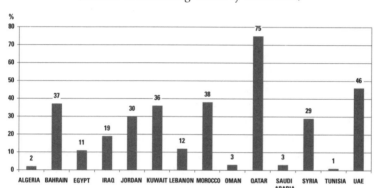

Al-Hurra's first aim has been set as the mobilisation of the Arab public in the same way as VOA mobilised mass movements in Poland and Eastern Europe during the Second World War (Pattiz 2004). Some have doubted the impartiality and integrity of Al-Hurra, however. Being under the BBG's strict guidelines, Al-Hurra has been criticised for being under the influence of the American government. Some have accused the channel of attempting to convert Arabs to American ideas (Wise 2005). In his discussion of the effective role of Al-Hurra, Pattiz has referred to the Arab print media's stiff resistance to the launch of the channel. Before Al-Hurra went on air, *Al-Khaleej* newspaper compared its launch to a military campaign. It called upon the US administration to change its policy in the region, if it hoped to refine its image across the Arab world. The fiercest attack on Al-Hurra came from the migrated print media (Lahlali 2009). *Al-Quds Al-Arabi* criticised the first interview the channel conducted with President Bush, claiming that the interviewer posed soft questions and was not aggressive enough in his questioning.[1]

The Egyptian weekly, *Al-Usbu'*, published an article in which it sharply criticised Mouafac Harb, Al-Hurra's former executive vice president and director of network news, calling him 'the first Arab Zionist' (Wise 2005). *Tishreen*, a Syrian newspaper, interpreted the launch of Al-Hurra as an attempt 'to re-colonize the Arab homeland that the United States seeks to implement through a carrot-and-stick policy' (Wise 2005). The sharp criticism of Al-Hurra could only be interpreted as being due to its association with the US government, whose Middle Eastern foreign policy was unpopular across the Arab world. In his response to the criticism, Mouafac Harb rejected the claim that the channel's impartiality and transparency suffer because of the funds it receives from the US government (Lahlali 2009). He defended democracy and considered it to be the cornerstone of Al-Hurra's practice. Harb was almost reiterating Pattiz's official line that the aim of launching the channel was to spread and promote freedom and democracy in the Middle East. Pattiz fervently believes that Radio Sawa and Al-Hurra could be the right vehicles to do this, and not to act as the voice of the Arab people in 'their grievances against Israel' and the United States. Al-Hurra's mission is manifested in 'the station's respect for its audience and message of personal empowerment [which] is in stark contrast to the messages of victimisation put out by the major government-controlled TV channels in the region' (Pattiz 2004: 79). American public diplomacy was the main reason for establishing Al-Hurra in the first place; the US government felt the urgent need to reach out to the Arab public and convey US policies in Arabic through an Arabic-sponsored channel. Not everyone, however, has been convinced that this new method of persuasion will bear fruit. Jon Alterman, Director of the Middle East Program at the Center for Strategic and International Studies, does not make any secret of his objection to Al-Hurra: 'I'm uncomfortable with the idea that in a very complete and relatively open news environment, I'm not sure of what the niche of Al-Hurra is' (Wise 2005).

Radio Sawa is described as having one of the largest Arabic-language radio news departments in the world, with correspondents and stringers across the Middle East (Pattiz 2004). While

Radio Sawa offers entertaining songs for the Arab youth generation, Al-Hurra focuses on news and information, devoting fourteen out of every twenty-four hours of transmission to news
(Pattiz 2004). Al-Hurra offers a wide range of programmes, but,
as will be discussed in the next section, some of its programmes
are not interactive enough to compete with channels such as
Al-Jazeera and Al-Arabiya. Despite Al-Hurra's attempt to appeal
to the Arab public through its programming, its ranking is still
very low in comparison with other Arabic channels. The stiff
competition from Al-Jazeera and other Arabic channels has meant
that Al-Hurra needed to rethink its programming and its relationship with the US government. Al-Hurra has made some progress
as far as its programmes are concerned. On 8 March 2009, the
channel launched its *Al Youm* (*Today*) programme, which airs three
hours of live coverage of news from five Arab countries across
three continents. According to Nancy Snow (2010) '*Al Youm* is not
a typical political hard news program that emphasizes dramatic
images and conflict situations. It is a hybrid style of news programming that offers breaking news, soft news, finance.' Snow
concludes that this programme, among others, has improved the
reputation of the channel and its image in the region. While some
in the Middle East still associate Al-Hurra with Bush's administration and its aim of spreading its propagandistic views, Snow
alluded to the fact that this perception started to fade away with
the arrival of Obama's administration. Snow remarks a shift in
both the channel's performance and its image in the region.

While Pattiz (2004) hails Al-Hurra and Radio Sawa as a success,
others consider the inception of Al-Hurra a failure because it was
unable to attract more than 1 per cent of the Arab public (Lynch
2004, 2006). Al-Hurra's lack of success is attributed to its programmes, which are described as 'boring, uninteresting' and 'out
of tune' with Arab audience interests (Rugh 2004). Al-Hurra's
programmes have been reviewed and revamped to meet the
demands of the Arab public, and the launch of *Al Youm* was
designed to counter those critics of Al-Hurra's programmes.

It is not only its programmes which have come under attack,
however; its judgement over the content to broadcast could not
escape criticism. In 2004, all Arab transnational channels covered
live the assassination of Sheikh Ahmed Yassin, Hamas's spiritual

leader, but Al-Hurra chose instead to air an American cooking programme translated into Arabic. The channel was not only criticised for this, but was labelled out of touch with the Arab audience. By choosing not to air the event live, Al-Hurra sought to please its sponsor (Lahlali 2009). For Al-Hurra to gain respect in the media market in the Arab world, it should cover the White House's politically sensitive issues (Snyder 2005). The channel's journalistic practices have also been under scrutiny. The interview with Bush after the Abu Ghraib scandal, in May 2004, was regarded as soft and lacking in aggressiveness. Despite the US government's optimism about Al-Hurra's achievement, the channel still has a long way to go to win over the sceptic Arab public. This public, which rejects US policy in the Middle East, will find it extremely difficult to embrace coverage from a channel subsided by the same government. Until the US government changes its policy towards the Middle East, the Arab public will always remain sceptical of any media organisation associated with it. The arrival of Obama's administration could be said to have helped Al-Hurra to penetrate the Arab market, but the daily reality of the conflicts in the region serves as a reminder to the Arab public that US governments are behind such conflicts. Despite its finest journalism and professional staff, Al-Hurra remains a victim of US government policies in the region. The unfailing support for Israel and the slow progress in resolving the Israeli–Palestinian conflict, coupled with the conflict in Afghanistan and Iraq, makes the Arab public suspicious of Al-Hurra's coverage. The 2006 conflict between Israel and Hezbollah, and the American public's vocal support for Israel, did not help to promote American values and foreign policies in the Arab world. As for Al-Hurra, these are the kind of events that it dreads most, as it finds itself in a difficult situation in attracting Arab viewers while adhering to the BBG's broadcasting international code of practice.

Pattiz (2004) paints quite a positive and optimistic picture of the role of Radio Sawa and Al-Hurra in cultivating the Arab audience, occasionally appearing very confident that Al-Hurra will achieve the same mission as that of VOA during the Second World War and the Cold War. One should not, however, lose sight of the fact that the US wars on Iraq and Afghanistan have spawned a sense of discontent with US foreign policy in the Middle East. This sense of unease among the Arab public about the war could serve as a barrier for Al-Hurra and Radio Sawa to achieving their main objectives in the same way as VOA did in Second World War. Andrew Kohut, director of the Pew Research Center for the People and the Press, refers how the war on Iraq has ignited anti-American sentiments in the region (Robinson 2005). As for Al-Hurra, its success depends on its programming and its way of dealing with Arab issues. Unless it demonstrates that it is capable of aggressively questioning American policies in the Middle East, and critically analysing American domestic policies, Al-Hurra will always be regarded to be serving its sponsor, the US government, and will not be able to win over the Arab public's hearts and minds (Lynch 2006).

Al-Hurra's programmes

Despite its attempt to provide refreshing programmes and innovative shows, Al-Hurra has found it extremely difficult to penetrate the Arab media market because of stiff competition from other Arab channels. The fact that it is a US broadcaster has raised suspicion among the Arab public. According to Rugh (2004: 3):

the content and style of the news gave the impression that it was not an Arab channel but American. Subjects that were chosen, and the time devoted to them in newscasts, seemed determined from an American point of view rather than an Arab perspective.

This has led Arab viewers to tune in to watch Al-Jazeera and Al-Arabiya instead (Rugh 2004). In its coverage of events in Iraq after 2003, the channel has been highly disappointing in its accuracy and effectiveness in disseminating news and information from the country, despite the fact that it has been supported and backed by the US government on the ground (Rugh 2004). Although this has given Al-Hurra more opportunities to access more places in Iraq than could other news broadcasters, Rugh (2004) argues that the channel has failed to capitalise on these. It should be said here, however, that Al-Hurra's reports have sometimes had an impact on the decision makers. For example, the channel's recent coverage of the lack of medical care and insurance for Iraqi soldiers who were injured while serving their country has led to the Iraqi government opening the first medical hospital for injured soldiers (Conniff 2010).

The other criticism directed towards Al-Hurra is that its programmes do not scrutinise American domestic issues in the same way as those of Al-Jazeera and Al-Arabiya do. Arab viewers expected Al-Hurra 'to cover the US domestic scene much better, more comprehensively than anything they had seen before' (Rugh 2004)[2]. However, Conniff (2010: 2) rejected these claims, insisting that Al-Hurra continues to offer a more thorough analysis of events involving 'US foreign policy to the Middle East than any other channels in the region'. He goes on to say that Al-Hurra provides an extensive coverage of US domestic affairs and refers to Al-Hurra's documentary series *Americans*, which offered a historical analysis of the origin of the American people and their history and included an insight of the history and culture of Arab-American people.

Al-Hurra's soft approach in dealing with Arab governments, and the issues of reform and corruption, have damaged its reputation. Its interview with the Tunisian foreign minister during Ben Ali's regime was aired after the channel agreed to drop any questions related to human rights abuses in Tunisia (Rugh 2004). As a free channel, Al-Hurra is expected to champion freedom of expression and human rights issues, but in this case it showed more interest in interviewing the minister than in questioning him about his country's human rights record.

The channel offers a wide range of daily and weekly programmes, including *The World Now, The World Today, Doors, In Iraqi, Global, Free Hour* and *All Directions*. The following brief description of the programmes is adapted from the channel's website where fuller details can be found (http://www.alhurra.com).

Al Youm, as mentioned earlier, is a three-hour programme that covers a wide range of topics and is contributed to by presenters from Dubai, Cairo, Beirut, Jerusalem and Washington, DC.

The World Now is designed to provide news updates from the Middle East, the United States and around the world. This news programme is repeated every hour.

Doors is a weekly round-up of cultural events in Iraq, with the latest news and interviews on exhibits, theatre, gallery openings and film festivals.

In Iraqi is an hour-long discussion programme from Baghdad. It examines the most up-to-date issues facing contemporary Iraq, with analysis and debate from Iraqi experts and politicians.

The World Today is a daily hour-long newscast providing reports from the Middle East and the rest of the world.

Global is a daily hour-long newscast providing reports from the Middle East, the United States and around the world.

Free Hour is one-hour weekday discussion programme that examines and analyses news and issues of the day.

All Directions is a round-table programme, which provides analysis, discussion and a review of the events of the past week, with newsmakers and experts on different issues. Each week, it examines the knock-on-effect of US policies on the Middle East and the rest of the world.

Very Close is an hour-long interview with an important Arab cultural figure, such as poets, writers and entertainers from the Middle East.

Sports Weekly examines the week's top sports news from the Middle East, as well as showing global highlights from a wide range of sports including soccer, baseball, rugby, tennis, basketball, hockey and other major sporting events. It also profiles some of the most influential and popular sport stars from the region and around the world.

In addition, Al-Hurra broadcasts documentaries from around the world on topics such as science, medicine, history, the arts and current affairs.

A close examination of the above programmes reveals that they are heavily focused on news. Although Al-Hurra's programmes are chiefly designed to promote discussion and debate about issues in the Middle East and the world, their scope of encouraging the Arab public to contribute to the debate is quite limited in comparison with Al-Jazeera and Al-Arabiya. Apart from its programme *Al-Hurra and the People*, which asks the same questions to different people across the Middle East, it offers no opportunity for the audience to contribute to live discussion. In addition to the news broadcast, Al-Hurra sought to break taboos and has managed to discuss the issues of gender equality and women's rights in two programmes, *Musawat (Equality)* and *Hunna (Women)*.

Al-Hurra's programmes and code of practice came under

criticism in 2006, when it was suspected that its journalists were not adhering to the standards and principles of US international broadcasting. Al-Hurra's coverage of a speech made by Hassan Nasrallah, Hezbollah's leader, prompted questions among the BBG as to whether the channel was adhering to its code of practice, and the same question was raised when one of Al-Hurra's reporters aired in December 2006 a short report on the denial of the Holocaust in a conference in Tehran. This has led to a thorough review of its broadcasting practices, as a result of which a new code was implemented that barred speeches or interviews of 'suspected terrorists' from being aired on the channel. The review also called for close supervision of the Arabic programmes. In response to this review, three daily editorial meetings were introduced to plan programmes and decide on the news and information to be aired. The channel also reviewed its training for its journalists, and put in a place a training package for them, to be carried out by the Missouri School of Journalism and the George Washington University School of Media and Public Affairs.[3]

Al-Hurra and the 1994 International Broadcasting Act

The 1994 International Broadcasting Act is considered as a guide for the BBG. The Act was modified in 2004 to the United States International Broadcasting Act 2004, and codified in the United States Code (22 USC Chapter 71). The code promotes freedom of expression which it considers as having some ground in the international law, mainly human right article 19.

The right of freedom of opinion and expression, including the freedom 'to seek, receive, and impart information and ideas through any media and regardless of frontiers', is in accordance with Article 19 of the Universal Declaration of Human Rights, section 302(1).

American international broadcasting law promotes freedom of discussion and debate; however, the new Act seems to tie journalistic objectivity to foreign policy goals. This entails that journalists should operate in a framework that ensures that the main foreign policy objectives are achieved, and consequently the channel's autonomy is somehow influenced by the BBG, despite the existing 'firewall' policy. Critics of Al-Hurra have used this to suggest that, like any other Arab channel, Al-Hurra is no different from the Arab state channels which promote and defend governments' policies.

Sections 303 and 306 of the Act state clearly that foreign policy should be the guiding principle for international broadcasting. This seems to be at odd with section 303(b)(1), which highlights that the BBG is responsible for producing 'news which is consistently reliable and authoritative, accurate, objective, and comprehensive'. The question to be posed here is: what would happen if Al-Hurra's coverage conflicted with US foreign policy? Rugh (2005: 86) cites the example of the Abu Ghraib incident, which undermined US foreign policy objectives. To be guided by foreign policy goals entails that the channel is under restrictions as to what it should broadcast.

The question that arises from such a practice is: how can Al-Hurra be objective while its content is determined by foreign policy goals? Some have argued that this makes it no different to the Arab state-controlled channels, which US governments often criticise for lacking accuracy and impartiality. I think the interference of any government in media affairs is a threat to the main tenet of freedom of the press and expression. Al-Hurra and other international broadcasters should be left free to broadcast outside the framework of government foreign policy.

The BBG is answerable to Congress, which uses its powers to discipline Al-Hurra for venturing beyond American policy. According to Youmans (2009), 'the law's effects, therefore, tell a different story, one of political stricture, ideological monitoring and other principles at odds with the promotion of democracy.'

Despite the Unite States government's insistence that Al-Hurra's broadcasting is objective and, like other international broadcasters, adheres to its foreign policies, others cannot find any disparity between the US codes of practice and other authoritarian systems, where the media 'support and advance the policies of the government' (Rugh 2004: 23). The difference between the two is that the US government tends to tacitly control the media through a set of laws and codes, while authoritarian regimes directly control the media to advance their agenda.

Al-Hurra's lack of autonomy has made the channel less popular among Arab viewers. Some consider it the mouthpiece of the American government. Such an attitude towards Al-Hurra has made it difficult for the channel to make a breakthrough in the Arab market. The most recent surveys suggest that the channel failed to win over the Arab public: a poll by Telhami and Zogby in 2007 indicated that only 1 per cent of the Arab public watches Al-Hurra as a first source of news, and their 2008 survey results showed 2 per cent of Arab viewers tune in to Al-Hurra for international news reporting (qtd in Youmans 2009).

Despite its attempts to appeal to Arab viewers, Al-Hurra remains the least viewed channel compared with Al-Jazeera and Al-Arabiya. Its website is accessed by only a small number of the Arab readership. Table 3.2 shows a breakdown of its readership by country.

Table 3.2 *Al-Hurra website readership distribution in May 2008. (Source: http://www.alexa.com, accessed 19 May 2008 and 8 January 2009, qtd in Youmans 2009)*

Country	May 2008
Yemen	3,130
Sudan	7,390
Saudi Arabia	11,956
Qatar	13,875
Egypt	17,310
UAE	19,391
Morocco	19,696
Algeria	23,199
Kuwait	23,888
Iran	64,387

Statistics released by the BBG in January 2010 show that Al-Hurra is making slow progress compared with Al-Jazeera and Al-Arabiya, and ranks in third place after them in most Arab countries. There are a host of reasons why Al-Hurra's viewership is low compared with those of Al-Jazeera and Al-Arabiya. The channel's association with the US government remains one of the main barriers for Al-Hurra to attract Arab viewership as the channel is often seen as a propaganda tool for the US government to promote American culture and values to the Arab world. Having watched some of its programmes, one cannot doubt the hard work and enthusiasm of some of its employees; however, as long as Al-Hurra is associated with the US government, it will always be regarded the mouthpiece of that government, no matter how professional its employees may be. The fact of the matter is that the channel could establish itself as a real contender to Al-Jazeera and Al-Arabiya if it was helped by the US government's foreign policy in the region.

Al-Hurra could attract more Arab viewers if some of its programmes provided viewers with the opportunity to contribute to the programmes through faxing or calling in. Its lack of call-in shows is one of its known weaknesses. Unlike Al-Jazeera, which provides platforms to its viewers to call in and express their opinions, Al-Hurra does not offer anything of the sort. Offering a platform for viewers to call in and express their views would, however, test the BBG's code of practice, as it would be extremely difficult to control incoming views, especially of those who expressed support for organisations seen as hostile to the United States.

Al-Jazeera seems to be taking the lead in interacting with its viewers through its website. In addition to the opportunity given to readers to comment on most of its online material, the channel allows readers to search and retrieve transcripts of the programmes aired over the last five years, free of charge. In contrast, according to Lynch (2004: 102), Al-Hurra 'has only a rudimentary and content-free Web site'. As stated earlier, Al-Hurra has been trying to be interactive with its readers and viewers; its daily segment *Al-Hurra and the People* is a step towards establishing an interactive line of communication with people across the Middle East (Conniff 2010). What sets Al-Jazeera apart from Al-Hurra and other channels in the region is its decision to offer a platform for viewers to call in and express their views live on air, some of which are often very critical of individual regimes and governments.

The difference between Al-Jazeera and Al-Hurra is not only in style and format, but also in the genre of discourse used to address controversial issues in the region. Chapter 4 is devoted to analysing the differences in the usage of discourse between Al-Hurra, Al-Jazeera and Al-Arabiya.

Criticism of Al-Hurra

Al-Hurra has been criticised for its programming. Lynch (2004: 102) points out that this has been 'tepid' and Al-Homayed (2004) remarks that 'anyone who knows the American media or has worked in Washington will be shocked watching this satellite channel broadcasting at its present standard'. Al-Homayed's comments are reiterated by many other Arab viewers who have expressed their discontent with the channel's programming. Lynch (2004: 102) summarised these views, saying 'I have heard its programs described as boring, tedious, stale, and – most damning – as no different from the programming found on the Arab state-run stations to which Al-Jazeera offered such a refreshing alternative.' Recent research, however, shows that Al-Hurra's programming is improving (Snow 2010). According to Conniff (2010: 1), Al-Hurra has developed 'ground-breaking programming and its journalists have consistently provided professional newscasts'. For Conniff, most criticism of Al-Hurra is out of date and does not reflect the current situation. The major criticism among viewers is that Al-Hurra offers programmes that are 'out of tune with Arab concerns' (Lynch 2004: 102). Al-Hurra has also come under a cloud of criticism for not critically covering American domestic policies; however, if Al-Hurra were to cover American domestic issues critically, it might find itself under heavy criticism from Congress. This, according to Lynch 2004, constitutes a dilemma for the channel, which cannot be solved by its programming or its talented staff. But, the biggest problem of all is the channel's reputation among the Arab audience. The channel has been regarded as an American channel that is used as propaganda to promote the US government's policies in the Arab world and beyond, and this has lost the channel its credibility among Arab viewers (Lynch 2004). During the Abu Ghraib scandal, the channel aired a documentary called *Remembering Saddam*, which was designed to show that what happened in Abu Ghraib was not as bad as what had happened during Saddam's rule. The documentary featured three men with amputated hands meeting

President Bush. To Al-Hurra's critics, the documentary was designed to deflect criticism of the United States over the Abu Ghraib scandal. Al-Hurra's timing of running this documentary could be interpreted as providing a sort of cover-up of the scandal.

Al-Hurra's initiative and response to the region's main concerns and political issues have been very slow, indeed sporadic at times. Unlike Al-Jazeera, which provides daily debate and discussion on Middle Eastern issues, Al-Hurra remains cautious about providing free debate on issues related to US government policies in the region. To borrow Lynch's words, 'Al-Hurra failed to become part of the Arab political conversation' (2004: 104). Al-Hurra's cautious approach has allowed other channels in the region to shine and compete with Al-Jazeera, the popular face across the Arab world. Al-Arabiya seems to have learned from Al-Hurra's mistakes by taking a bold broadcasting stance, similar to Al-Jazeera's. Recent research on the channel, however, shows that Al-Hurra is making progress and some of its programmes, such as *Al Youm*, are seen to have added value to the channel's programming. Snow (2010), for example, concludes that the change in the US administration has helped the channel to cement its position, and also considers that the launch of *Al Youm* has helped the channel to gain some legitimacy.

Al-Arabiya

Al Arabiya was launched on 3 March 2003 as a news broadcaster that was considered a real competitor to Al-Jazeera in the region, 'a channel Riyadh has disliked ever since it went on air in 1996, rankled by investigative reports on corruption in many Arab countries and the airing of Osama bin Laden video statements' (Cochrane 2007). Al-Arabiya's primary vision is to provide an alternative Arab news outlet governed by 'reasoned and responsible freedom', without being engulfed in the controversies often associated with its rival Al-Jazeera (Zayani and Ayish 2006). Sheikh Walid al-Ibrahim, a Saudi, is the owner of Al-Arabiya. His main goal is to establish Al-Arabiya as a calm and objective news broadcaster.

Al-Arabiya started with a large number of reporters in different Arab and non-Arab countries. Its coverage includes politics, business, current affairs, finance, sports and science. Like Al-Jazeera, Al-Arabiya launched talk-show and call-in programmes, and encouraged debate and discussion online. The channel is managed by another Saudi, Abdul Rahman Al-Rashed. In 2004, Al-Rashed stepped down as editor of *Asharq Al-Awsat*. He was immediately approached by Sheikh Walid, who encouraged him to join the channel. Al-Rashed is known for his fierce opposition to Islamic fundamentalism and other Arab media in the region (Al-Saggaf 2006: 2). The arrival of Al-Rashed brought with it a few editorial changes; correspondents, for instance, started referring to American troops in Iraq as 'multinational forces', and not as 'occupying forces' (Al-Saggaf 2006: 2). Al-Rashed's vision has been to create a channel in which space is carved out for liberal ideas, and he has often talked about the necessity of providing balanced coverage of events. He considers his approach to be totally different from that of Al-Jazeera, which, because of its critical approach and sharp journalism, 'run[s] into trouble with virtually every Arab government' (Hammond 2007: 3). Under Al-Rashed's guidance, Al-Arabiya shifted away from blaming the United States for the invasion of Iraq, to providing documentaries on the pre-invasion human rights abuses in Iraq. This has been regarded as an attempt by the channel to contextualise the invasion and provide a balanced account of what is going in Iraq. Salah Najem, Al-Arabiya's first news editor-in-chief, stressed the channel's commitment, saying it would offer:

> News with quality production and editorial values, as well as a look on the screen and the provision of opinions that respect the reason and mentality and dignity of both the audience and our guests and provides a broad range of opinions, rather than going for the easy solution. (Feuilherade 2003)

However, some consider the channel's new shift in strategy to be an attempt to appease the Americans that has nothing to do with impartiality in its broadcasting. The new shift has also been seen as an approach to 'undermine the insurgency' which was widely supported by Iraqis (Hammond 2007). Although the Iraqi interim government expressed its discontent with both Al-Jazeera's and Al-Arabiya's coverage of the events in Iraq, Bush chose Al-Arabiya over Al-Jazeera to give an exclusive interview about the Abu Ghraib incident. This strengthened the sceptics' view that the new channel was created to serve the American agenda in the region. Islamists' websites refer to Al-Arabiya as 'al-'ibriya' ('the Hebrew channel').

The launch of Al-Arabiya was designed to rival Al-Jazeera, which has been very critical of Saudi society and government. Some consider Al-Arabiya as an alternative to Al-Jazeera; however, the fact that it is owned and managed by Saudis has raised suspicion among others, who question its ability to cover Saudi domestic affairs impartially. In fact, some suspect the channel to favour the Saudi government in its coverage. Since its inception, the channel has shown the ability to provide solid coverage of events of the same quality as that of its opponent, Al-Jazeera. According to Al-Saggaf (2006: 3) 'Al-Arabiya is known not only for its ability to offer instantaneous reporting and coverage of major events, but also for setting new standards in the application of new technology to the world of television.'

Al-Arabiya has been particularly critical of those championing Arab nationalism and political Islam, both of which have been regarded as a threat to the Kingdom of Saudi Arabia. A review of the history of Arab nationalism shows quite vividly the tension between Gamal Abdul Nasser, the champion of Arab nationalism, and the Saudi government at the time. Al-Arabiya's stance against Arab nationalism could be said to have been influenced by the Saudi government, which has long stood against Gamal Abdul Nasser's ideas. Similarly, some consider Al-Arabiya to have taken the same line as the Saudi government when dealing with Islamists. The Saudi government expressed its commitment to fighting extremist views, especially those calling for the overthrow of the Saudi regime for its collaboration with the West. When Al-Jazeera aired a series of interviews with Mohamed Hassanein Heikal, confidante of Gamal Abdul Nasser, who talked about Arab nationalism and the era of Gamal Abdul Nasser, Al-Arabiya responded by airing a series called *Ayyam al-Sayyid al-Arabi* (*The Days of Mr Arab*) in 'an attempt to discredit this ideology of resistance to Western hegemony' (Hammond 2007: 5).

According to Al-Saggaf (2006), what sets Al-Arabiya apart from other Arab news channels is its 'sophisticated production values' and 'its high-tech look'. However, objectivity, impartiality and the quality of the delivered product should constitute the main criteria in differentiating between the channels. Al-Arabiya has proven that it could be a good rival of Al-Jazeera, but it has still to cover a great deal of ground to catch up with its opponent. A joint University of Maryland and Zogby International poll of viewers in Saudi Arabia, Morocco, Jordan, Egypt, Lebanon and the United Arab Emirates found that Al-Jazeera led with 65 per cent of respondents saying they view Al-Jazeera more than Al-Arabiya, while 34 per cent said they viewed Al-Arabiya more than Al-Jazeera (Hammond 2007). Al-Arabiya's viewership has increased since its launch. As the statistics in Table 3.3 show, the channel enjoyed a surge of viewership, especially in Iraq, Kuwait and Saudi Arabiya.

Table 3.3 *Al-Arabiya's viewership distribution.*
(Source: Youmans 2009: 56)

Country or global region	Estimated households watching	Estimated potential pudience
GULF		
Bahrain	75,900	500,680
Iraq	397,000	1,573,000
Saudi Arabia	678,760	5,920,850
Kuwait	240,000	1,072,000
Oman	30,200	141,400
Qatar	70,650	359,250
UAE	91,600	530,200
Yemen (North & South)	89,600	450,800
MEDITERRANEAN		
Algeria	599,000	2,576,000
Cyprus	1,050	4,600
Israel	89,489	357,956
Lebanon	17,038	67,152
Morocco	2,544,500	9,578,000
Tunisia	38,928	161,712
Turkey	17,980	69,920
West Bank & Gaza Strip	650	2,600
Total	**4,982,345**	**23,396,120**

Al-Arabiya's programmes

Al-Arabiya provides a wide range of programmes, including politics, culture, sports and arts. The following brief description of the programmes is adapted from the channel's website, where fuller details can be found (http://www.alarabiya.net/en/aa_programs.html).

Dhaif wa Ḥiwār is a sociopolitical talk show dealing with current affairs. It involves discussions with guests, including decision makers, about issues related to their own countries. Interviews are often carried out by the local correspondent in the country where the guest is based or via satellite from Dubai.

Ṣabāḥ Al-Arabiya is Al-Arabiya's morning show, where news, sports news, and social and cultural issues are briefly presented in a lighter format.

Ṣināʿat al-Mawt deals with the issue of global terrorism. It considers the topic from different angles, taking into account different religious, economic, social and political explanations of this phenomenon. The show invites guests and known experts in the field to comment on different topics related to the subject.

As-Sulṭah Al-Arābiʿah reviews the international print media in the United States and Europe. The show focuses on coverage of importance to the Arab audience. International journalists are hosted to comment on the coverage of the international media, and the show also provides an insight into the major differences in journalism between different cultures.

Bi-Ṣarāḥa hosts high-profile guests, such as heads of states, government ministers and business leaders. The show discusses social and political issues related to the Middle East.

Nahāyat Al Usbūʿ provides a review of the main highlights of the week. It invites experts to review major press reports on key issues from across the region.

Min al Irāq is a sociopolitical programme which highlights ordinary Iraqis' daily lives, raising awareness of the major difficulties facing them. The show also invites Iraqi decision makers to comment on different social, economic and political topics in Iraq.

Bil Arabi is a live sociopolitical talk show in Arabic. It hosts high-profile guests who are seen to have played a big role in decision making. The show consists of two parts: the first part focuses on the guest's career and the major decisions made; the second part discusses current affair issues with the guests, and their impact both regionally and internationally.

Fil Marmā covers everything to do with the world of football. It provides reviews of the day's best games and keeps the audience up to date with the latest news and information about the most famous players, but also focuses on the achievements of clubs, individual players and various national teams.

Aswāq al-Iraq deals with Iraq's general economic situation from different angles.

Anaft wa Al-Ghāz presents viewers with the latest news with regard to the exploration, drilling and processing of oil around the world and in the Middle Eastern region. It also provides information on global changes in oil prices.

Akhir Sāʾa is a detailed news bulletin that covers and analyses the day's biggest news stories in depth.

Panorama provides an in-depth discussion of current political, economic and social affairs.

Rawāfid takes the viewer into the lives of interesting cultural and artistic icons, including poets, writers, musicians, film makers and historians. It discusses the impact the work of these icons has on our minds and daily lives.

Muhima Khāsa is an investigative programme that seeks to uncover the truth about a wide range of social, religious and political issues. It digs deep into each story, uncovering the secrecy surrounding the topic.

Iḍaʾāt is a sociopolitical talk show with the Gulf Cooperation Council as its point of focus. It hosts prominent figures from the Arab region to discuss topics of public interest.

Mahaṭāt reports three untold stories from three different societies. The stories can be of a social, cultural or political nature.

The above description shows that Al-Arabiya has a variety of programmes that cover a wide range of issues; however, one cannot help noticing some overlaps. There is a tendency by the channel to cover specific issues related to specific countries, and this might make some of its programmes of little relevance to other Arab viewers. The focus on Iraq in more than one programme may make the channel look like an Iraqi national channel. The issue of Iraq could be integrated in other programmes such as *Panorama*, for example. There is also a lack of programmes on women and their contribution to the society.

Al-Arabiya's programmes are designed to rival those of Al-Jazeera. Its high-tech approach and its endeavour to cover the middle ground often exposes the channel to criticism for adopting a soft approach when it comes to critical matters such as American foreign policy and Arab regimes. For Al-Arabiya, exercising caution in the coverage of events is part of a balanced approach to broadcasting; however, this approach came under fire when Al-Arabiya was critical of Hamas during the Israeli assault on Gaza.

Similarities and differences between the three channels

It could be said from the above discussion that Al-Jazeera, Al-Hurra and Al-Arabiya are three main channels that have been established to serve a common purpose, that is free, impartial and transparent news broadcasting. However, a close examination of their broadcasting strategies, programmes and code of conducts reveals that there are visible differences between the three channels. These differences stem from the willingness of every individual channel to make its mark on the Arab audience by demonstrating its ability to champion freedom of expression. Their coverage of events differs quite extensively from each other. But before dwelling on the different features distinguishing each channel, let us examine some of their common features.

The three channels are supported by different sponsors. This might have some impact on the way the channels deal with their sponsors in their broadcasting. For instance, Al-Jazeera has been heavily criticised for not being critical enough of the Qatari government and regime. While it remains active and critical of other Arab regimes, the channel adopts a silent approach towards its sponsor.

The same could be said of Al-Hurra, which is sponsored by the US government. Al-Hurra's broadcasting has to adhere to the international broadcasting code of practice, which is designed to keep the channel in line with US foreign policy. A violation of this code has led, as has been discussed above, to reviews of the channel's broadcasting practice. Like Al-Jazeera, Al-Hurra has also been criticised for its soft approach when dealing with US domestic issues and some have accused the channel of not doing enough to explain American domestic issues to the Arab public. The channel has also come under heavy criticism because of its approach of not covering events related to groups or organisations which are deemed a threat to US safety and security.

The same charges have also been filed against Al-Arabiya. Although it covers issues related to Saudi society, it has expressed little criticism of the Saudi regime. In fact, Al-Arabiya has been very cautious of taking on any Arab government or regime. It is worth mentioning here that Al-Arabiya, since its launch, has benefited from hosting senior US officials. For example, President Barack Obama gave his first interview to an Arabic channel to Al-Arabiya in January 2009 (Kraidy and Khalil 2009). Obama's interview has boosted the channel's profile in the region but despite this, the channel is still rated second to Al-Jazeera in most Arab countries.

The three channels have different strategies when it comes to their broadcasting approaches. Al-Jazeera's approach is to appeal to the Arab public through covering issues that are related to them. Its coverage of the Palestinian issues and the war on Iraq and Afghanistan has proved to be popular among the Arab public. Its strategy of offering a platform to the voiceless has strengthened its presence in the Middle East. Its new call-in programmes have made the channel accessible to the Arab public. But, it is its constant criticism of US foreign policy that has most increased the channel's popularity among the Arab public. The channel's approach of covering news from an Arab perspective has cemen-ted its position in most Arab countries. It has proven popular because, first, it credits the Arab public's actions and often dis-credits their governments; second, it offers its audience news and information in line with their thought. Judging from its viewer-ship, this is a successful strategy and the Arab public will tune in to Al-Jazeera because they believe it to be a credible source of news.

As for Al-Hurra, its approach is quite different. While it strives to promote freedom of expression in the region, the channel's approach of promoting US government policies in the region has proved to be counter-effective. Its coverage of the events in the region is seen not to be aggressive enough, and often not to the Arab public's taste. Its programmes, though colourful they may be, do not encourage the Arab public to get involved and express their opinions. The call-in programme shows, which have become very popular among the Arab public, are yet to be introduced by Al-Hurra. Some consider this as an attempt to limit the Arab public's involvement in debates and discussions of importance to them.

Unlike Al-Jazeera and Al-Hurra, Al-Arabiya's approach is to provide a balanced coverage of events without upsetting any party. One of its aims is to avoid any coverage that would create division and enmity among the Arab countries, a practice that Al-Jazeera has been accused of. This approach has been put into the test, however, especially during Israel's 2008 assault on Gaza. The channel was very critical of Hamas, and partially blamed them for the escalation of the conflict. This did not go down well with the Arab audience. The channel has also been charged with promoting discord between the Sunnis and Shias (Cochrane 2007).

As the above discussion demonstrates, the three channels have different characteristics which set them apart from each other, but it is fair to say that all three have a long way to go to gain complete independence from their sponsors. Their achievement should be celebrated and their newly adopted broadcasting style in the Middle East should be encouraged. Meanwhile, they should not shy away from holding governments and organisations accountable for their actions.

Conclusion

Over the course of this chapter, I have introduced Al-Jazeera, Al-Hurra and Al-Arabiya. I have discussed their objectives, sponsorship, codes of practice and their programmes. I have highlighted the major issues that make each channel distinctive from the others. Al-Jazeera's approach of fearing no one gains the channel popularity among the Arab public, but makes it unpopular among Arab regimes and some Western governments, namely the United States. Despite its endeavour to provide free and transparent coverage, the channel has stopped short of achieving this goal because of its loyalty to the Qatari government. But this should not detract from the argument that Al-Jazeera has been a pioneer in bringing a critical approach to Arab journalism.

Al-Hurra's objectives, however, are slightly different from those of Al-Jazeera. Its inception was not only intended to promote freedom and democracy in the Middle East, but to improve and refine the United States's image in the region. Its programmes are rich, but, unlike Al-Jazeera, they are not open to the public to express their opinions. The channel's code of practice is seen to restrict its coverage of events that could be of great interest to the Arabic public, as the channel cannot cover anything that conflicts with its main foreign policy. Also, the perception of some of the Arab public that this is a US channel makes it difficult for Al-Hurra to gain more ground in the Arab media market.

Al-Arabiya's broadcasting approach is similar to some extent to that of Al-Hurra. Both were launched as a counter-attack to the hegemony of Al-Jazeera, therefore they both seem to be against the notion of Arab nationalism and Islamic fundamentalism; however, they differ in the way they approach international issues. Al-Arabiya is more open to providing a platform for people of hostile views to the US government than Al-Hurra will do. Unlike Al-Hurra, Al-Arabiya runs call-in shows, where the audience is invited to take part in the discussion.

Despite the differences in their broadcasting approaches and their strategies, the three channels aspire to provide fair and transparent coverage to the Arab public. They might have different styles, but they have the same aspiration of promoting freedom of expression in the Middle East.

Chapter 4

The Arab Media and the Discourse of Conflict

The aim of this chapter is to provide an in-depth textual analysis of the coverage of the conflict between Hezbollah and Israel in 2006. Based on this analysis we will try to establish the inextricable link between language and the socio-cultural and political ideologies that contribute to the production of discourse. Some of these ideologies are represented through language. Language as a means of communication can be used to influence opinion and change readers' attitudes, especially during conflicts. Such an influence could have a great impact on the way we perceive others, and could have detrimental effects on the harmony of different groups or different nations. In this chapter, I will shed some light on the theoretical frameworks which underpin my analysis. Examining the coverage of the conflict from a critical perspective will enable us to unravel the social, cultural, political and ideological motives behind the production of discourse.

I shall compare and contrast the usage of language by the three Arabic channels, Al-Jazeera, Al-Arabiya and Al-Hurra, and provide a textual analysis of language extracts from the three channels which will take into consideration different contextual factors that contribute to the production and consumption of discourse. I will draw on critical discourse analysis (CDA) as a framework for my analysis of the discourse practices of the above channels. The following section introduces the reader to the phenomenon of discourse analysis and critical discourse analysis.

Definition of discourse

The development of discourse analysis has been the subject of debate over the last two decades. As the focus of linguists shifted away from sentence structure towards the meaning of the sentence and its context, the debate gathered momentum. Much work has been done to refute Harris's notion of discourse, which focuses mainly on the level and structure of discourse (Widdowson 2004), but the main debate has centred on the difference between discourse and text. According to Wallace Chafe (1992, 2003), 'text' and 'discourse' can be used interchangeably:

> the term discourse is used in somewhat different ways by different scholars, but underlying the differences is a common concern for language beyond the boundaries of isolated sentences. The term text is used in similar ways. Both terms may refer to a unit of language larger than the sentence: one may speak of a discourse or a text. (Chafe 1992: 356)

Chafe's views have ignited debate on the difference between discourse and text.

Widdowson (2004), on the other hand, holds completely different views. He rejects the idea that the text is a stretch of the language beyond the sentence. According to Widdowson, the text can take the form of a word, a clause or even a letter, but discourse is the interpretation of the text in a specific context. Widdowson has been supported by other scholars in emphasising that the context is at the heart of discourse, and it is the context which makes discourse more interactive, involving the producer and consumer of discourse. It is the act of interpretation of the text by the recipient which makes a text a piece of discourse (Lahlali 2007). Some have gone even further to look at how discourse shapes and is shaped by society (Candlin 1997). This brings us to critical discourse analysis.

What is critical analysis?

Critical analysis is rooted in theories of power and ideology pioneered by Foucault (1977, 1981), Habermas (1984) and

Bourdieu (1977, 1988), who placed the emphasis on discourse in society. The critical analysis of discourse has taken different linguistic forms such as critical linguistics, critical language studies, critical discourse analysis and critical language awareness (Lahlali 2007). CDA practitioners consider the function of language to be the main pillar of critical studies (Fowler et al (1979), Hodge and Kress (1979, 1988, 1993) and Fairclough (1989, 1992a, 1992c)). Similarly, Halliday (1973, 1978) stipulates that language shapes our surrounding: 'Language is as it is because of its function in social structure, and the organisation of the behavioural meanings should give some insights into its social foundations' (1973: 65). Language is not considered just as a tool for conveying information but it can serve our understanding of the society in which we live. It can shape our culture, social behaviour, power and organisation. This is embodied in Fairclough's methodological approach, which he considered as 'an orientation towards language [which] highlights how language conventions and language practices are invested with power relations and ideological processes which people are often unaware of' (1992c: 7). In his definition of CDA, Fairclough said:

> By critical discourse analysis I mean analysis which aims to systematically explore often opaque relationships of causality and determination between (a) discursive practices, events and texts, and (b) wider social and cultural structures, relations and processes; to investigate how such practices, events and texts arise out of and are ideologically shaped by relations of power and struggles over power; and to explore how the opacity of these relationships between discourse and society is itself a factor securing power and hegemony. (1993: 135)

Fairclough, however, goes further to declare that power is practised tacitly. He states that it 'is implicit within everyday social practices which are pervasively distributed at every level in all domains of social life' (1992a: 50). It is accepted that CDA explores the connection between daily talk and the production of, maintenance of, and resistance to systems of power, inequality and injustice (Fairclough 2001). Van Dijk (1998) makes clear the position of critical discourse analysts, by saying that 'critical discourse analysts take an explicit position, and thus want to understand, expose and ultimately to resist social inequality'.

Why CDA and media discourse?

During the 1980s and 1990s, most researchers of media discourse chose CDA as their framework to approach these studies (Zidan 2006). This is because CDA focuses on the social and political aspects of media texts and also enables us to approach other disciplines while analysing media texts. Van Dijk's analysis of media discourse, for instance, places a great emphasis on the production and consumption of discourse, both of which shape and are shaped by social practice. Van Dijk (2000: 36) postulates that:

> media discourse is the main source of people's knowledge, attitudes and ideologies, both of other elites, primarily politicians, professionals and academics. Yet, given the freedom of the press, the media elites are ultimately responsible for the prevailing discourses of the media they control.

Similarly, in his definition of CDA, Fairclough placed the same emphasis on social equality.

According to van Dijk (1998: 2–4), several requirements need to be observed if CDA is to fulfil its ultimate aims. These requirements are reflected in his belief that CDA can go beyond the surface structure of discourse to show how discourse conceals relations of power and inequality, and how it is often being ideologically shaped (Lahlali 2007). Van Dijk's requirements constitute the core of Fairclough and Wodak's (1997) main tenets of CDA, which can be summarised as follows:

1. CDA addresses social problems.
2. Power relations are discursive.
3. Discourse constitutes society and culture.
4. Discourse is historical.
5. The link between the text and society is mediated.
6. Discourse analysis is interpretative and explanatory.

7. Discourse is a form of social action.
8. Discourse does ideological work.

Although Fairclough and Wodak's tenets are essential to this study, the main focus will be on the last one. In my analysis of the discourse of the three main channels, I will try to figure out the main difference in the way discourse is produced and ideologically influenced. By doing so, I intend to show how, through discourse, people and organisations can express their beliefs, identities and ideologies. Mumby and Clair (1996: 183) make this clear by pointing out that:

discourse analysts are using the notion of ideology in a particular fashion. The term refers not to ideas, beliefs that individuals take on, but rather to the process by which social actors, as part of larger social collectives, develop particular identities and experience the world in a particular way.

Fairclough and Wodak (1997) maintain that text and society are inextricably linked; therefore, in order to understand a piece of discourse, one needs to examine the text in relation to its social, cultural and wider global context. It is the time and space of the production of the text that can at times help us make sense of the elements behind its production. According to Fairclough (1989), ideas do not come from free heads, by which he means that ideas are ideologically loaded.

Who produces and consumes media texts?

The production of media texts (news reports, media stories) goes through management stages. Media organisations are responsible for the collection, selection and editing of the text to be produced (Bell 1991, Silverstone 1985, van Dijk 1988, Fairclough 1995). Many professional media producers are behind the final production of media texts, including journalists, editorial staff and technical staff. It could be said that the production of media texts is a collective effort (Fairclough 1995). A news story, for instance, will go through several checks to ensure it is newsworthy and does not contravene the organisation's broadcasting policies. The final products are often in line with the organisation's broadcasting beliefs and ideologies. According to Fairclough (1995: 49), the production of media texts can be 'seen as a series of transformations across [. . .] a chain of communicative events which links source events in the public domain to the private domain consumption of media texts'.

The nature of the products depends on the media organisation itself. Although media organisations often claim their impartiality in the compilation of news stories, nevertheless their beliefs are often tacitly embedded in the production of texts. This, again, depends on the political orientation of the media organisation itself – conservative, liberal, state-run, and so on. In the Arab world, the disparity in the narration of the story reflects the media's political orientation. As we shall see from the data below, different channels use different discourse lexemes to convey their message. As a result, the story is conveyed through the organisations' lenses and broadcasting beliefs. What is judged to be a 'terrorist' in one media organisation is considered a 'freedom fighter' in another. Such a disparity, which can be traced back to both cultural and political beliefs, makes the story an interesting piece of news that is reported and transformed in line with each organisation's sets of beliefs.

Any media text is constitutive of the producer's social identity, social relations and systems of knowledge and belief (Fairclough 1995). But the question here is: how does this affect readers and viewers? According to van Dijk (1991), in order to understand and explain what happens when readers read news and digest information, we need to apply a cognitive approach. He argues that socially shared knowledge and cognitive principles are constrained 'by personal, situational, and more general social and cultural constraints of understanding newspaper reading, and mass communication' (van Dijk 1991: 42). The interpretation of media texts may show a big variation among readers and viewers who might belong to different classes and cultures, and have different levels of education (van Dijk 1991). These viewers or readers often adopt an active approach when processing news and information, however; the process of filtering news and information is strategic. Van Dijk (1991) mentions that one of the strategies used by readers of media texts is to understand the overall meaning and content of relevant media texts without dwelling on details related to structure and linguistics. Van Dijk points out, however, that for a full understanding of news and information, readers simultaneously combine information from 'different structural levels and sources at the same time, in a "parallel" fashion' (1991: 229). This enables readers to understand the information by referring to the context of production and their personal knowledge about society and culture; however, such analysis will be limited to those elite or educated categories of society who have the linguistic ability to understand and interpret news. In the Arab world, for instance, the high rate of illiteracy would make such analysis and interpretation of content impossible, therefore not all readers or viewers would be able to apply van Dijk's strategy of news processing. What is striking about van Dijk's strategy of news processing is the empowerment of the reader to reproduce the information from his or her own perspective, considering the context of the news.

Although van Dijk (1991) focuses on the cognitive aspects of understanding and processing information, like Fairclough, he insists on the salient role of context in understanding the meaning of a text. The new transnational Arab media seems to be aware of such a context in the production of news and information. It produces news and information from a Middle Eastern perspective. The use of language, as will be discussed later in this chapter, reflects such a strategy.

Fairclough's framework

As stated above, in this chapter I shall draw on Fairclough's (1995) framework in my analysis of the data. This particular framework is chosen because it enables the text to be located within its social and cultural context.

Fairclough stipulates that every piece of discourse has three main dimensions: a text, both written and spoken; a discourse practice, which involves the production and consumption of texts; and a social action. According to Fairclough, 'the discourse practice dimension of the communicative event involves various aspects of the processes of text production and text consumption. Some of these have a more institutional character, whereas others are discourse processes in a narrower sense' (1995: 58).

Discourse practice is a mediating channel between the text and social and cultural practice. Elements of sociocultural practice shape the text, but by way of shaping the discourse practice (Fairclough 1995).

The notion of sociocultural practice considers the wider national and global social and cultural practice. By looking at sociocultural practice, we can unravel the wider issues that shape the text, by way of discourse practice. This will be extremely relevant to our analysis of the three channels' practice, with a particular focus on the national, regional and global cultural and political preposi-tions which shape their production of discourse.

Although linguistic analysis is intended to cover elements of sentence structure, grammar and so on, the main focus of the analysis should be on the selectivity of lexis, which, I believe, reflects opinions, beliefs and values. Most media organisations express their values and beliefs through the production of media texts. As alluded to above, the text shapes and is shaped by these practices. The selection of lexical items can have a wider implica-tion on the consumer of the text; it can mobilise, arouse feelings of anger and can lead to social actions. Utilising, for instance, the word 'extremist' rather than 'religious man' to address a neigh-bour might have some implications on the relationship between neighbours (Zidan 2006); it might have some knock-on effect on the established trust between them. The analysis of these lexical items should take into consideration the context of their produc-tion, as this helps in explaining the main reasons behind a particular choice of lexical item.

In addition to examining the choice of lexical items, I will also examine what is often referred to as 'naming strategy'. This involves names and labels given to particular individuals, groups and cultures. The naming strategy reflects the values and beliefs of the text producer. The naming strategy is often used to create 'particular propagandistic ideologies, or stereotypical images which are part of opinion expression' (Zidan 2006: 86).

Attribution strategy will also be used in the analysis of media texts. This includes the qualities, features and attributes assigned to individuals, groups, organisations, societies or cultures. The attribution strategy can serve as a clear indicator of the producer's stance, values and beliefs.

Going back to Fairclough's framework, one cannot cease to observe the centrality of the text in any aspect of media discourse. The analysis of media text takes different forms, including detailed analysis of 'visual images and sound effects' (Fairclough 1995: 33). Text analysis should also bring together linguistic analysis and intertextual analysis. The emphasis should be on the fact that the text is hybrid and contains different genres and discourses. Text analysis therefore should accommodate all levels of sentence analysis, as well as the wider social and cultural aspects that might affect the text. Fairclough (1995) asserts that the relationship between the text and society should be seen dialectically. This means that the text shapes and is shaped by society.

The consumption of news and information can differ from one culture to another. Readers and listeners of certain cultures interpret and make sense of the news in relation to their prior knowledge or schemata. Arab and Muslim viewers process information based on 'repertoires of schemata' that are deeply entrenched in their culture and religion (Barkho 2006). These cultural cues are paramount to the interpretation of media texts, and Arab readers tend to draw on them in the meaning and understanding they attach to news. This entails that any news item or media text is interpreted against the cultural backdrop of the reader or listener. This might constitute a challenge to writers or reporters, who should be familiar with the culture of the people to whom they are reporting. Their news and information should match the expectations of the reader or viewer. This expectation is often deeply rooted in the culture or tradition to which readers or viewers belong. Meeting readers' expectations, however, raises several questions pertaining to the objectivity and transparency of producing a piece of discourse. The dilemma that faces journalists and reporters is how to balance their reporting in a way that ensures impartiality and the wider dissemination of information among readers and viewers of different backgrounds. Most journalists, reporters and media organisations are aware that their success is judged, not only by how widely their work is disseminated and accepted, but by the impact it has on the consumer. In Western culture, the ratings issue pushes journalists and reporters to make an effort to attract as many viewers as they can.

As alluded to in Chapter 3, the reason why Al-Hurra has not

managed to break through the Arab media market is because of its association with the US government, therefore its influence remains limited and the trust of Arab viewers in the channel is not that great. Al-Jazeera's contrasting approach is clearly reflected in the following quote from its managing editor, Waddah Khanfar:

> Arab political and security issues – the events in Palestine and Iraq – seize the attention of most of our viewers. Programs tackling Muslim judicial and religious issues also come at the forefront of topics our viewers are interested in. Al-Jazeera satellite channel attempts to provide a comprehensive, objective and balanced news and information service of the issues that attract the attention of our viewers. (Barkho 2006: 7)

Although the CDA approach appears to be appropriate for the analysis of media texts, many scholars have expressed their doubt about it. Widdowson (1995, 2004) criticises CDA for its vagueness in drawing a clear line on many issues. For instance, he points out that there is no clear distinction between 'discourse' and 'text'. He considers the usage of discourse to be both 'vogue and vague' (Widdowson 1995: 158). He also criticises CDA for its reliance on the interpretation of texts rather than the analysis of them. In his view, such an approach serves the practitioner's political agenda, and therefore lacks objectivity. He charges CDA practitioners with using their ideological stances to 'derive from the text the discourse which fits their preconceived ideological commitment [. . .] it presents a partial interpretation of text from a particular point of view' (Widdowson 1995: 169). He claims that the interpretation approach should be replaced with a thorough analysis of discourse to ensure objectivity in the analysis. He alleges that CDA practitioners are often selective in their analysis, and that only items and issues that fit well with their agenda are selected to support their argument: 'What we find frequently in CDA work, then, is essentially a pretextual partiality of interpretation which is given the appearance of analytic rigour' (Widdowson 2004: 109). But Widdowson's main criticism is of CDA's framework of analysis. The different methods of analysis within CDA have been questioned by some CDA practitioners, who have called for a standardised method for the analysis of the text. Fowler (1996) and

Toolan (1997) have called for a review of CDA's methodological approach, with a view to developing a comprehensive method that can be used by all CDA practitioners.

Even CDA's critics, however, acknowledge that CDA has offered a substantial contribution to discourse analysis (Toolan 1997; Widdowson 1996, 2004). CDA should be credited for its approach of linking discourse to change, and its impact on social and cultural practice. It has helped practitioners to unravel social justice, racism, hegemony and discrimination. Also, CDA has been credited with providing solutions to and taking action on issues analysed or examined by CDA practitioners.

Content and representation in news reports

Over the last few years, as mentioned in Chapter 1, the Arab media has witnessed an unprecedented proliferation of outlets, some of which are private and others state-owned. Different media outlets have their own formats and styles that set them apart from each other. Culture and language are two main distinctive features that distinguish the international media from each other. Such differences are clearly visible in the ways in which issues are reported and represented. But differences can be noticed even among media that speak the same language and belong to the same culture, due to their political orientation, values and beliefs. These values are often represented in the type of discourse employed such as naming, labelling and representation of other issues. As a result of these practices, some media outlets have created stereotypical images about certain groups, cultures or places (Zidan 2006).

Language as a means of communication can be exploited to give a false representation of the world surrounding us. Any misrepresentation could have a dire consequence for the level of human relations and cultural divergence. Misrepresentation not only causes certain cultures to be viewed as inferior to others, but often creates stereotypical images that can diminish the other. The act of looking down on groups, individuals and cultures in media often occurs in times of conflict, where these cultures and people are looked at as the enemy who deserves no respect, and the media often transfers the political messages of its governments or organisations.

In his analysis of racism in discourse, van Dijk (1991) considers 'perspective' to be one of the important features of discourse. By perspective, he refers to the point of view from which events and actions are described. Van Dijk concedes that the notion of perspective remains elusive because it is difficult to pinpoint how writers identify themselves with one group or another. He argues, however, that a selection of items of discourse implies an opinion and often reflects the writer's beliefs and school of thought.

Van Dijk (1991) regards perspective in semantic discourse to be both a local and a global feature of semantics. He states that a perspective is not confined only to the selection of words and sentences, but to the way people and their actions are represented in the text (van Dijk 1991). Fairclough (1992b) makes a similar observation when referring to the production of discourse. He points out that discourses shape the political and ideological perspectives of their producers, either overtly or covertly.

The interpretation and explanation of implicit meaning in the text remains one of CDA's main tasks. The discourse we consume today is often stuffed with ideas, which more often than not reflect the producer's beliefs and knowledge. The text is a mine of information, where only a small proportion of meaning is expressed explicitly in words and sentences (van Dijk 1991, Fairclough 1995). This leads us to consider the question of how to detect implicit meanings in media texts. Language is rich with its lexis and structures, and meanings can be expressed explicitly by the way lexis is selected and sentences are formed. The selection of lexis, as mentioned earlier, can contain some inferred knowledge and information. The following example from van Dijk (1991: 181) illustrates this clearly:

The West Indian women claimed that they were being discriminated against.

The use of 'claim', according to van Dijk, implies that the West Indian women might not be telling the truth. Instead, for instance, of using the verb 'said', the journalist chooses to cast some doubt on their statement. Such a doubt undermines both the statement and the person making this statement.

Here is another example, which sheds more light on the implicitness, or often implied meaning, in news reports:

> [A] member of the parents' action group organized the chanting among the children and encouraged them to run away from the school gates, *probably for the benefit of television cameras*. (*The Times*, 17 September, in van Dijk 1991: 182)

For van Dijk the use of the statement 'probably for the benefit of television cameras' implies that the whole action is staged and that cameras were already in place to record such an event. This also implies that the event had been planned in advance and that cameras had been put in place to publicise it. The use of the verb 'encouraged' indicates that the children's action was not innocent, but perhaps influenced by a member of the parents' action group. Such a discourse could be seen to play down the children's action and express doubt about the spontaneity of their action. But the question here is: what motivates the producer to use such a type of discourse? Perhaps the text producer was against the action, or perhaps held different beliefs to those organising it.

Ideologies are most often embedded within the implicit meaning of a text (Fairclough 1995). The analysis of representation in a text takes several forms. Analysing themes, such as war, necessitates going beyond the traditional 'microanalysis', which itself is a very useful method of analysis, but alone does not paint a complete picture of what is intended in that piece of discourse (Fairclough 1995). The microanalysis could be supplemented by a content analysis to give an overview of what is happening in the text, as well as what is excluded from it. To borrow Fairclough's (1995) terminology, we need to examine what is present in and absent from the text. Although Fairclough and van Dijk used different terminologies to refer to what is said and unsaid in the text, both seem to agree here that the text constitutes 'said' and 'unsaid' elements of discourse.

The notion of 'us' and 'them' in discourse is often elaborated on to demonstrate different strategies by speakers to polarise opinion. In their analysis of Bush's speech after September 11th, Leudar, Marsland and Nekvapil (2004) demonstrate how Bush has used different semantic terminologies to draw a dividing line between the attackers and the United States. In his speech, Bush employed the first plural pronoun 'our' to refer to the citizens of the United States: 'our way of life' and 'our freedom'. His speech was addressing two groups, the citizens of the United States, representing the first plural pronoun 'our', and the attackers referred to as 'them'. Although the second group was not identified at this stage in Bush's speech, the attributes of the group were quite clear. They were 'evil', 'despicable' and 'the enemies of the United States'. The use of phrases such as 'mass murders' and 'evil' were aimed at rallying the citizens of the United States behind their leader and nation.

Bush's description later was used to characterise people of Arab and Middle Eastern decent (Merskin 2004). These descriptions were picked by the media who reinforced this stereotype of 'monolithic evil Arabs' (Merskin 2004). The language used by the media in the news, as well as in movies and cartoons, has reflected this sort of stereotype directed against a certain group. Hall (1997: 258) points out that stereotypes 'get hold of the few simple, vivid, memorable, easily grasped, and widely recognised characteristics about a person, reduce everything about the person to those traits, exaggerate and simplify them, and fix them without change or development to eternity'. But the most worrying issue is that the image conveyed in the media is that 'all Muslims are Arabs' and all Arabs are 'terrorists' (Merskin 2004: 158). So both the media and political leaders, Bush in this case, have constructed a stereotypical image of Arabs as enemies. This inaccurate representation by the media of certain groups can have a devastating effect on these groups, who might feel targeted and marginalised in the society in which they live. Many Americans of Middle Eastern descent have complained about this stereotype and how it has impacted on their lives. So the presentation of particular groups in a bad light in the media can reinforce certain stereotypes and images held by ordinary people. In this case, the media can and should be held responsible for constructing an inaccurate image of the group. Some media, especially in time of conflicts, build on political leaders' opinions and rhetoric, and broadcast their propaganda without questioning their motives. History has taught us that political leaders use the idea of a 'common enemy as a method of social control, of reinforcing values of the dominant system, and of garnering participation in the maintenance of those beliefs' (Merskin 2004: 159).

Discourse, representations and power

Representations in clauses or sentences

I follow Fairclough's definition of 'discourse representation', which means 'speech reportage' (1995: 118). This means that the representation of events, actions, cultures and people can be accomplished through different ways. Not only do producers of these events have a wide range of choices in terms of vocabulary to represent what they describe, but their selection of lexis and their choices can reveal their identities and beliefs. Fairclough (1995) gives the example of how violent death at the hands of others can be represented in completely different ways, depending on the motives of the producer. It might be called 'killing', 'murder' or 'massacre'; others might call it a 'holocaust' or 'extermination' (Fairclough 1995: 109). In addition to the selection of vocabulary to represent a piece of discourse, the use of grammar can also be revealing in terms of how events are represented, and from which perspective. The use of active and passive voices to describe events can not only determine who said what, but can give an insight into why agents of the verb are made explicit or implicit. To illustrate the use of the passive voice, Fairclough (1995) gives the example of a comment by a guest on BBC Radio 4's *Today* programme. The guest commented on the 'cheap' Russian fish being dumped on British markets, saying: 'the funny thing is it's not transferring itself to the consumer at terribly low prices at all'. The speaker here has omitted to refer to who has transferred the fish and who is responsible for the price. The agents for both actions have been elided; such a representation of the actions may have significant ideological effects on the reader (Fairclough 1995).

Jusiæ (2009: 32) holds the same view, stating that any selection and 'production of information within media institutions are consciously or unconsciously guided by frames that organise the belief and knowledge system of journalists and editors'. He refers to Goffman's (1974) model when analysing his media discourse in reference to the conflict in former Yugoslavia. Goffman's theory of framing has been the subject of discussion and analysis, and various researchers, such as Entman (1993), have contributed to its development. Entman defines the theory as follows:

> Framing essentially involves selection and salience. To frame is to select some aspects of a perceived reality and make them more salient in a communicating text, in such a way as to promote a particular problem definition, causal interpretation, moral evaluation, and/or treatment recommendation for the item described. Typically frames diagnose, evaluate, and prescribe. (Entman 1993: 52)

Based on the theory of framing, Entman produced four locations that could help in the analysis of media. These include selection and production of discourse; culture and wider sociocultural context; source of information; and selection of facts, and the way things and actions are represented and presented to the reader or the audience. The frame is also seen to help the receiver to process and interpret the information received. This is based on the receiver's knowledge, beliefs, identity, experience and individual needs.

It should be mentioned here that Entman's four locations are similar to what Fairclough presented in his media discourse framework. What sets Fairclough's framework apart from Entman's is its emphasis on textual analysis as a means to unravel the social, cultural and ideological factors that can often surround the text. Fairclough (1995) and others have discussed extensively the process of text production and consumption. They have also discussed in great detail the role of semantics in conveying one's ideological and political stance. Although Entman's model has the basic features of the analysis of media discourse at a time of conflict, still I believe it lacks detail in its analytical approach, a concept that Fairclough has put at the heart of his framework.

Since this chapter examines the coverage of three Arab channels of the 2006 conflict between Hezbollah and Israel, it would be useful to refer to some of Jusiæ's proposed discursive strategies. Jusiæ (2009: 340) mentions four main discursive strategies of representation that were used by the media as a framework for explaining the conflict: inventing enemies; inventing victims; a historicisation; and hiding real problems/silencing.

These strategies constitute the framework through which the media bases its coverage. By adopting some or all of these strategies, the media can have total control over how to present the conflict to the reader or viewer. Its coverage certainly shapes the nature of the debate. It has ultimate power and control over who should be given a platform and who should not. Although in the modern age, the media is supposed to provide a balanced report for readers and viewers, it can still exclude certain groups, individuals and indeed governments from its coverage, often giving unconvincing justification for its actions.

As mentioned in Chapter 3, Al-Hurra was reviewed by the BBG for broadcasting a speech by Hassan Nasrallah, Hezbollah's leader, who is labelled by the US government a 'leader of a terrorist organization'. The exclusion of Hezbollah from the conflict means that the whole conflict will be covered from one perspective. By tarnishing Hezbollah as a terrorist organisation, the media have shaped the nature of debate, and sought to inform the public of the ills of Hezbollah. Through such a practice, the media have often sought to mobilise the public against the 'enemy' in the conflict. Selecting the enemy in a conflict can have a multifunctional purpose. It can lead to presenting the enemy as 'an obstacle, the opposite, an existential threat and, thus, the political target towards which the force of the attack is turned' (Markovic 1997: 27). It can rally the public and create a homogeneous public sphere, with the sole aim of taking collective action in order to defeat the enemy. The danger of such homogeneity is that it often marginalises other groups who might oppose the media's action, or who might have different opinions to the mainstream media. One of the main concerns about the media creating a homogeneous public is that it gives the political elite an outright mandate to act freely and without restriction. In addition to contributing to the creation of a homogeneous public that could unreservedly support politicians, the media can play the role of 'hiding problems/silences'. Jusiæ (2009) refers to the coverage by some media of the conflict in former Yugoslavia, where the discourse of nationalism and patriotism took precedence over objectivity and balanced coverage. Some of the media has gone even further to incite hatred and discrimination against particular groups in order to 'maintain the stability of authorities' (Jusiæ 2009: 36). So, the media as a channel of communication has turned into a powerful propaganda tool exploited by the government to mobilise the public to support its agenda. The chief aim of this strategy is to create the concept of 'us' against 'them', bringing any opposition or dissidents into line with the government.

To avoid being trapped in governments' insistence on nationalism and patriotism, the media ought to uphold the basic media principles of freedom, transparency and fairness. One of the main tenets of media is to raise awareness of certain aspects of society, such as human rights. The media also has a major duty of giving a voice to those voiceless people who are often silenced by the powerful elite, or who have been deprived by the state's media of the opportunity to express their opposing views and opinions. Journalists have a duty to monitor human rights abuses, and proactively engage in examining all aspects of society that have an impact on citizens.[1]

The control of the operation of the media by owners, editors and executives often undermines journalists' attempts to provide a fair, representative and transparent piece of information. As a consequence, the public is often exposed to inaccurate or distorted information, which can be used to form opinions and attitudes towards certain events, groups or actions. The control of the media discourse often narrows the debate and kills different arguments, which could contribute to the enrichment of society.

Reporting conflicts is a very sensitive issue, and reporters and journalists should report ethically in order to deliver balanced, impartial and fair information to the public.[2] Distortion of any information will only fuel the conflict and create further confrontation between different citizens or states. It is therefore the role of the media to try to defuse conflict and not to fuel it. Al-Jazeera, for instance, has been criticised on numerous occasions for airing graphic images of civilians who fell victim to conflict. Some regard Al-Jazeera's action as a means of fuelling the conflict, but Al-Jazeera has rejected this charge.

With journalism comes responsibilities. It is the responsibility of every journalist to ensure his or her integrity is not, in any way, compromised; their independence and objective reporting is their main objective in disseminating news and information. The following section will thoroughly examine some of the extracts from both Al-Jazeera and Al-Arabiya's coverage of the Hezbollah–Israel conflict in 2006, and attempts to show how reporters and journalists represented the conflict to readers and viewers.

Method of the study

Data of the coverage of Al-Jazeera, Al-Arabiya and Al-Hurra of the Hezbollah–Israel conflict were collected for the period 12 July to 14 August 2006. Some of the data is in the form of news items, documentaries and discussion shows, and some featured on the channels' websites. The war lasted for 34 days, and ended with United Nations Security Council Resolution 1701, guarded by a multinational force. Most of the international and Arab media called this the sixth Arab–Israeli war. Some Arab media expressed their support for Hezbollah, while others tried to strike a balance in their coverage. The following section will examine the three channels' coverage of the war. The focus will be on their selectivity of lexis, their sentence structure and their naming and labelling strategies. The content analysis will be contextualised and linked to the channels' main aims and objectives, as well as their strategies.

As alluded to in Chapter 3, although the three channels under study are Arab channels, each of them has its own sponsorship, policies and agenda. It is to be expected that each would offer a different explanation for the conflict between Hezbollah and Israel in 2006. The aim of this section is to analyse extracts taken from the three channels' coverage of the conflict. The focus of this analysis will be mainly on the selection of lexis, repetition of certain key terms, labelling, and reported and direct speech (that is, narratives and voices).

Representation of voices in the three channels

In this section, I would like to focus on how the three channels represented the voices involved in the conflict, dwelling mainly on the channels' impartiality or lack of it in dealing with these voices.

In a report entitled 'Battles and incursions', Al-Jazeera referred to a statement by Hezbollah stating that it had repelled an incursion into the towns on the borders of Israel:

The Islamic resistance affiliated with Hezbollah said that it has repelled an Israeli incursion in towns on the borderline shortly before midnight. In a statement, the Islamic resistance said that it has 'destroyed a Zionist warship Saar 5 off the cost of Sur'. It considered its action as a revenge for the martyrs of Qana. (1 August 2006)

Throughout its coverage of the war, Al-Jazeera followed a similar pattern by referring to the parties in the conflict whenever it stated gains, strong resistance and fierce fighting. Parties were interviewed and where possible statements were referred to:

The Israeli army threatens to demolish ten buildings in Lebanon for every missile launched on Haifa. (24 July 2006)

Al-Jazeera tried to strike a balance in its reporting by referring to both parties in the conflict; however, in its representation of voices involved in the conflict, two main themes emerged: hope and optimism, strong will and defiance when representing Hezbollah; frustration, setback and military power when representing the Israeli army. Hezbollah's optimistic vision and strong determination to defeat the Israeli military was manifested in the discourse of defiance delivered by its leader Hassan Nasrallah. In his speech to the Lebanese people, which was broadcast on Al-Jazeera, Hezbollah's leader promised a victory over the might of the Israeli military. He also assured the Lebanese people that Hezbollah had not been weakened and that it had the capability and power to hit Israel harder. Such a message, which was seen by some as a propaganda weapon to rally the Arab public and Lebanese people to support Hezbollah, was well received on the Arab street. The speech turned Hezbollah's leader into an Arab hero who had the audacity to take on Israel and inflict losses and damage on the reputable Israeli army. His focus on the gains his fighters had achieved isolated those voices who were against the action by Hezbollah which had triggered the conflict. In his 'victory speech' to a rally in Southern Lebanon, Hezbollah's leader invited the participants to celebrate what he called 'a divine victory': 'Let us renew our covenant and declare our joy at the divine victory to the whole world.' He then urged his supporters to be positive and forget about the past defeats: 'the time of victory has begun and the time of defeats has gone'. In his speech, he intended to promote himself as a leader who, for the first time in history, stood up and 'defeated' the Israeli army. The choice of lexis such as 'divine victory' was intended to show that the war with Israel was a holy war, conducted by 'Islamic fighters'. By resorting to a religious discourse, the Hezbollah leader was appealing not only to the Arab public, but to all Muslims across the globe.

Similarly, the Israeli voices often reassured their public of their military might and their ability to crush Hezbollah:

The Israeli Prime Minister, Ehud Olmert, announces that Israel is on the verge of achieving its aims and objectives. (August 2006)

Like Hezbollah, the Israeli government used the media to deliver its core message that it had the military superiority to disarm Hezbollah and weaken its ability to launch missiles into Israel. In a speech to army reserves, Ehud Olmert said on Al-Hurra:

21 days into the war and Hezbollah is no longer able to threaten the Israeli people. We will not accept a cease-fire until we see drastic changes on the ground. (1 August 2006)

The Israeli military's confidence was dealt a blow, however, when one of its warships was hit by Hezbollah. Also, the slow advance of the Israeli army on the ground meant that the military was making slow progress. As a consequence, doubt and unease engulfed the Israeli public, and the ability of the military to achieve its set objectives was called into question by many Israeli citizens. This uncertainty is represented in the following extract taken from Al-Arabiya's website:

In a comprehensive report for *Asharq Al-Awsat* newspaper, Nadir Majli discussed the Israeli response to the war, and the way the conflict was handled in Bint Jbeil. The report referred to Israeli television having said that Israelis have started believing the Hezbollah leader more than they believe their own leaders. (27 July 2006)

Two public voices emerged from the coverage of the conflict by the Arab channels: the Arab and Lebanese voices, which rallied around Hezbollah, convinced by its achievement in the war; and the Israeli public's voices, which cast doubt on the ability of their leaders to achieve the main objectives set at the beginning of the conflict. The three channels reflected these voices in their coverage. The only difference between them was that Al-Jazeera's representation of the Lebanese voices focused on their dismay and discontent with the level of destruction inflicted by the Israeli army, while the same voices expressed their support of Hezbollah and its leadership. Al-Arabiya, however, tried to maintain a balanced approach by representing voices that criticised Hezbollah for starting the conflict:

> An anonymous man said, 'I am not sure if Hezbollah was right when they caused this escalation; however it is not acceptable for Israel to cause this scale of destruction and kill civilians in this way.' (14 July 2006)

From the outset of the war, Al-Arabiya was very critical of Hezbollah. The channel often reminded its readers and viewers of who was responsible for the eruption of the war. It repeatedly pointed to Hezbollah for abducting two Israeli soldiers and killing others. By contrast, it was rare for Al-Jazeera to go back and remind its audience of the cause of the conflict; however, it is worth mentioning here that Al-Jazeera explained quite comprehensively the reasons for the war at the beginning of the conflict.

All three channels referred to the discontent of some of the Israeli public about the war. In a news bulletin on 1 August 2006, Al-Hurra referred to the Israeli civilians who had fled their homes in Northern Israel because of 'Hezbollah's missile attacks on crowded civilian areas'. Under the heading: '400 Israeli intellectuals condemn the Israeli "war crimes" in Lebanon' (2 August 2006), Al-Arabiya aired the intellectual voices that were against the conflict. The channel was very careful in representing their speeches, however; for instance, it directly reported the phrase 'war crimes' to distance itself from the demonstrators' action. Al-Jazeera, though, referred to the continuation of protests against the war. The channel adopted a generic form in reporting the demonstrations and protests inside and outside Israel:

> the continuation of protests against the Israeli aggression in Lebanon, and the call for an immediate cease-fire in Moscow, Lyon and Marseille in France. (31 July 2006)

> Hundreds of protesters demonstrate outside the defence ministry in Tel Aviv in the first wave of protests against the war on Lebanon. (31 July 2006)

These voices that were given a platform on Al-Jazeera and Al-Arabiya expressed their strongest criticism of the war and called for an end to the killing of civilians on both sides, but the brunt of the anger was directed to the Israeli government for allowing its military to cause civilian casualties.

Al-Hurra also represented these voices, though it focused mainly on the Israeli public voice that expressed anger at Hezbollah's action. It exerted a lot of effort to represent all voices involved in the conflict but the US and Israeli voices seemed to feature more heavily in its broadcasts than in those of Al-Arabiya and Al-Jazeera. Hezbollah's voice was often represented, based on statements released by Hezbollah. In Al-Hurra's news bulletin on 1 August 2006 and afterwards, the Israeli voice featured heavily through interviews and coverage of speeches made. Al-Hurra covered former Israeli Prime Minister Ehud Olmert's address to military graduates; it also featured an interview with the Israeli defence minister and a statement by Shimon Peres, President of Israel, who had visited the United States; and it ran an interview with a White House spokesperson. The Israeli voice in the channel was represented as strong, confident and superior. The heavy presence of the US voice and that of its ally Israeli exposed the channel to accusations that it was the mouthpiece of the US government.

The diplomatic voices of the international community were also represented on these channels, but there was a degree of disparity in the way in which this was done. All channels represented the United States as the strongest ally of Israel and which diplomatically was not willing to call for a cease-fire until Hezbollah had been disarmed. The American government voice was very critical of Hezbollah and its supporters, Syria and Iran, as this report from Al-Jazeera illustrates:

> Bush condemned in his weekly address the Syrian and Iranian role in the conflict, and said that they pose a threat to the entire Middle East. (23 July 2006)

The international community represented on the channels ranged from those who were against an immediate cease-fire to those who were calling for an immediate end to the war. The US and British governments were represented as the voices who were working to delay any cease-fire, to give the Israeli army ample time to crush Hezbollah; however, in an interview with CNN, the Secretary of State, Condoleezza Rice, denied this claim. Al-Hurra referred to the European voice as split down the middle on how to stop the conflict. While the British government's position was to urge both sides to stop the fighting, Spain and others called for an immediate cease-fire.

Al-Hurra also referred to the Iranian voice when covering the Iranian foreign minister's visit to Beirut. The channel considered Iran the strongest supporter of Hezbollah:

> The Iranian Foreign Minister announced his country's support for Hezbollah. (August 2006)

The selection of lexis

The three channels' coverage of the war reflects to some extent a similarity in the content reported, but there is a wide difference in the selection of lexis to convey meanings. For instance, Al-Jazeera referred to Hezbollah fighters as Islamic fighters or resistance, as in the following extract:

> The Islamic resistance affiliated with Hezbollah said that it has repelled an Israeli incursion in towns on the borderline shortly before midnight. (1 August 2006)

By describing Hezbollah as Islamic resistance, Al-Jazeera gave Hezbollah an Islamic legitimacy, consisting of representing Islamic nations and engaging in a holy war. Al-Arabiya, on the other hand, referred to the organisation as fighters, but what is striking about Al-Arabiya's labelling is the description of Hezbollah as a Shiite party. This was repeated in several reports:

The Shiite Hezbollah launched long-range missiles of Ra'd 1 type on Northern Israel which has led to the killing of an Israeli civilian. (13 July 2006)

An American official accompanying Bush to Germany said, 'We should remember that the conflict start with Hezbollah **(the Shiite)** launching missiles on Israel across the border, and abducting two Israeli soldiers.' (13 July 2006)

The question that one might pose here is: why did Al-Arabiya describe Hezbollah as a Shiite party? As mentioned in Chapter 2, Al-Arabiya is a Saudi-sponsored channel, and it is to be expected that its reporting would conform to the Saudi stance, which supports the Sunni practice. One interpretation of the description of Hezbollah as a Shiite party is that it was an attempt to erode the support it enjoyed across the Arab world, the majority of which is Sunni. The Saudi stance in the war was not clear from the outset. Some accused the Saudi government of allying with the American government in opposing Hezbollah but this was rejected by the Saudi foreign minister, speaking on Al-Jazeera:

Pan-Arab efforts to stop the war, and Israel continues its defiance The Saudi foreign minister, Saud al-Faisal, said that consultation between the Arab foreign ministers to hold a meeting in Lebanon is in progress. He insisted on the importance of finding a unifying stance to face this real catastrophe [. . .] in a comment on the doubt cast on the position of Saudi Arabia in the crisis, he said that nothing troubled the conscience of his country, and that Lebanese people are content with the stance of his country. He added, 'We have nothing to apologise for with regard to our position.' (2 August 2006)

In its coverage, Al-Hurra refers to Hezbollah fighters, but what is striking about the channel is its attribution of 'Lebanese' to Hezbollah:

> The **Lebanese** Hezbollah said it has forced the Israeli military to retreat. (1 August 2006)

The second choice of lexis which might strike readers when examining news reports from Al-Jazeera, Al-Arabiya and Al-Hurra is terminology such as 'martyrs' or 'martyrdom'. When the term appeared on Al-Arabiya, it was directly reported and used in quotation marks in an attempt to show the channel's impartiality, in conformity with its strategy of providing fair and balanced reporting. Al-Jazeera, however, adopted a completely different strategy by indirectly reporting speech, and in this case the word 'martyrs' was not directly reported. The following example from both channels demonstrates this clearly:

> A big photo of Hezbollah's leader, Hassan Nasrallah, was displayed along with photos of **'martyrs'** who have fallen in the war with Israel. (Al-Arabiya, 17 July 2006)

> In a statement, the Islamic resistance said that it has 'destroyed a Zionist warship Saar 5 off the cost of Sur'. It said this comes as a revenge for the **martyrs** of Qana. (Al-Jazeera, 1 August 2006)

Al-Hurra often used the term 'dead' or 'killed' when referring to casualties on both sides:

> Yesterday, the encounter between Hezbollah and Israel has led to the death of 828 Lebanese. (1 August 2006)

The description of the conflict itself is very revealing about the channels' positions and strategies in covering it. While Al-Arabiya described the Israeli war on Lebanon as 'a campaign' against Hezbollah, Al-Jazeera referred to it as an 'aggression', while Al-Hurra, on the other hand, opted for 'confrontation'. The choice of lexis here is very revealing. By choosing the term 'campaign',

Al-Arabiya sought to minimise the magnitude of the conflict; Al-Jazeera, however, opted for 'aggression', which, in Arabic, reflects the magnitude of the conflict, and presents the Israeli army as the aggressor. Al-Arabiya referred to the conflict as an Israeli campaign on numerous occasions, except once when it described it as an 'aggression':

> The defence minister, Amir Bertis, [*sic*] ordered on Wednesday the launch of **an aerial campaign** on Lebanon, targeting Hezbollah's establishments and the Lebanese infrastructure. The channel said that the **campaign** came in response to the abduction of two soldiers and the killing of others in a raid launched by Hezbollah today. (12 July 2006)

> Before the issuing of the United Nations resolution on Friday evening, Israeli officials announced that the army will continue its **military campaign** with the aim of ending the missile attacks launched by Hezbollah. (12 August 2006)

Al-Jazeera, however, describes it as an invasion and aggression:

> The current **invasion** is the fifth Israeli invasion of Lebanon in less than a quarter of a century. The killing of civilians and destruction remain the main common features of these wars. (20 July 2006)

> A public demonstration outside the United Nations and European Union headquarters in Beirut in protest against the **Israeli aggression** has called for an end to the siege and the war. (20 July 2006)

Throughout the coverage of the conflict, Al-Hurra referred to it as the 'confrontation' between Hezbollah and Israel. By choosing 'confrontation' to refer to the war, Al-Hurra put Hezbollah and Israel on an equal footing:

> The details of **the confrontation** between Hezbollah and Israel. (August 2006)

Peres ruled out the escalation of **the confrontation** with Hezbollah into a regional war. (August 2006)

Another difference that characterised Al-Jazeera, Al-Arabiya and Al-Hurra was the way they referred to the fallen dead on both sides. Al-Jazeera often used the word 'massacre' to describe a collective killing, while Al-Arabiya used the term 'massive killings'. Al-Hurra mostly referred to them as 'fallen dead'. Let us consider first the following examples from Al-Jazeera:

> The Lebanese envoy for the United Nations called for an urgent resolution, which should call for a cease-fire, and start the investigation into the **Israeli massacres**. (30 July 2006)

> Israel committed a **massacre** in the region of Ghaziyeh, South of Saida, resulting in a death toll of 14 civilians, including women and children. (8 August 2006)

> The Israeli army committed a new **massacre** in Nabatieh in the South of Lebanon by launching a missile which struck two family houses, resulting in the death of 9 members. (25 July 2006)

The word *majzara* ('massacre') in Arabic connotes a brutal action of the massive killing of innocent people.

Al-Arabiya, on the other hand, referred to both sides' actions as 'killing', except in the incident of Qana, which it describes as a 'massacre'.

Al-Jazeera's coverage of the conflict focuses mainly on the humanitarian side of the war, demonstrating how thousands of Lebanese people fled their homes seeking a safe refuge away from the intensive Israeli strike. The channel also focused on the level of destruction and demolition incurred on the country's infrastructure, which was reflected in its language usage. It often referred to the attack in terms such as: 'massacre', 'destruction', 'inhumane', 'innocent people are killed', 'nothing is spared', 'aggression' and 'war crime'. This type of language was designed to show the magnitude of the damage or loss inflicted by the Israeli army. Al-Jazeera's choice of language was designed to give it the edge over its rivals, who showed caution in the coverage of the war, and subsequently to appeal to Arab viewers who expected the channel to cover the conflict from an Arab perspective. Some of Al-Jazeera's critics accused the channel of compromising objectivity in an attempt to woo the Arab public.

Al-Arabiya, however, appeared to be cautious in its coverage from the outset. Although it criticised the Israeli action and the repercussions it had on civilians, Al-Arabiya often reminded its viewers that the action had been prompted by the kidnapping of two Israeli soldiers by Hezbollah fighters. In its description of the destruction of the infrastructure, Al-Arabiya used less strong language than Al-Jazeera. It used 'campaign', 'killing', 'suffering of civilians', 'scores of dead'. Al-Arabiya's coverage of the war reflects its approach of being a 'moderate channel'. Some, however, might accuse the channel of having being influenced by the Saudi government, which took an anti-Hezbollah stance.

Like Al-Arabiya, Al-Hurra was very cautious of its coverage of the conflict. On 1 August 2006, one of its reporters referred to the incident in Qana as the 'recent development in Qana'. Unlike Al-Jazeera, which kept referring to the incident in Qana as a 'massacre', Al-Hurra preferred to refer to it as 'recent development'. Some might accuse Al-Hurra of playing down the magnitude and scale of the deaths in Qana caused by the Israeli army. On the other hand, Al-Jazeera could be accused of fuelling angry sentiment among the Arabic public by referring to the incident in Qana as a 'massacre'.

Naming and labelling

The three channels have followed different strategies in naming and labelling activities, actions and events related to both Hezbollah and Israel. Hezbollah is labelled or referred to as 'Islamic resistance' and 'Hezbollah fighters' by Al-Jazeera, while Al-Arabiya often refers to Hezbollah as 'the Shiite party', and Al-Hurra refers to it as 'Hezbollah of Lebanon' and 'Hezbollah fighters' (see Table 4.1).

Table 4.1 *Differences in naming and labelling across the three channels.*

Al-Jazeera	Al-Arabiya	Al-Hurra
Israeli aggression	Israeli military campaign	Israeli military operation
Israeli massacre	Israeli massacre, Israeli killings	Killings
Islamic resistance	Shiite fighters	Hezbollah fighters
Martyr	Killed, 'martyr'	Killed
Destruction on a large scale	Destruction	Destruction, damage
Thousands of dead	Scores of dead	Deaths
Killed	Dead	Dead
Hezbollah launches missiles	Hezbollah waged missile attacks	Launched missiles, waged missiles
Immediate cease-fire, put an end to the military action	Put an end to the killing between Hezbollah and Israel	Put an end to the confrontation by both sides
The start of the war on Lebanon	The start of the conflict	The start of the confrontation
Elements of Hezbollah, Hezbollah fighters	Hezbollah fighters	Elements of Hezbollah, Hezbollah fighters

Table 4.1 shows the difference in the selection of lexis and the labelling and naming, which, as mentioned above, reflect each channel's political orientation and policy. While Al-Jazeera often resorts to Islamic religious discourse in describing the actions of Hezbollah, such as 'the Islamic resistance' and 'martyrs', Al-Arabiya tends to distance itself from this type of discourse by selecting secularist lexis to convey meaning. It refers to Hezbollah's killed fighters by using the Arabic verb 'killed' instead of 'martyr', and often the word 'martyr' appears between

parentheses if it is directly reported. This means that the 'scare quotes belong to an outside voice' (Fairclough 1995: 119), in this case Hezbollah.

It becomes quite evident from the selection of lexis that the channels choose the discourse that is often in line with their policies and sponsors' guidelines. For instance, Al-Arabiya played down the Israeli military action and its impact on both civilians and Lebanese society. In its coverage, it described Hezbollah as a power to rival the Israeli military. The use of terms such as 'Hezbollah wages missile attack' and 'the killings between the two' was designed to demonstrate that both Hezbollah and Israel were on equal footing. The same was reflected in Al-Hurra's coverage of the conflict. The use of 'confrontation' was intended to portray equity between the two sides. Al-Jazeera, however, described Hezbollah as the victim and the underdog which had taken on a military super-power. Al-Jazeera tried to show Hezbollah as victimised, while Al-Arabiya tried to hold it responsible for the escalation of the conflict. Al-Arabiya here put itself at risk of losing its Arab viewers, the majority of whom sympathised with Lebanon. During the first days of its coverage of the conflict, Al-Arabiya was heavily criticised for not supporting Hezbollah. Some labelled the channel 'al-'ibriya' ('the Hebrew channel') because they believed it supported Israel.

What we have here is three different approaches employed by three Arabic channels. First, an approach of appealing to Arab viewers by covering the conflict from an Arab perspective, which results in the increase in popularity of the channel, and subsequently an increase in its viewership. This approach was manifested in Al-Jazeera's reporting and coverage of the conflict. The second approach is to remain faithful to your sponsors and run the risk of losing some of your viewers, who might think that the channel is siding with 'the enemy'. Both Al-Arabiya and Al-Hurra found themselves in the awkward position of reporting the conflict in a way that pleased their sponsors but might upset their viewers. Al-Arabiya, for instance, was very keen on taking its sponsor's side. Al-Saggaf arrived at a similar conclusion when he stated that 'since Al-Arabiya is owned and managed by Saudis, it is possible that some of what is broadcast is intended to serve the interests of the government' (2006: 18).

Al-Jazeera considered the conflict an Israeli–Lebanese conflict, rather than Hezbollah–Israeli conflict. The channel also contextualised it by referring to other historical encounters between Israel and Lebanon. A historical reference was given to the reader or viewer to explain that this conflict was part of a series of conflicts that had engulfed both parties, even before the formation of Hezbollah. Al-Jazeera here tried to remind its readers that this was a pattern followed by Israel, and the recent conflict was not something new. The aim of this was to shift away the blame from Hezbollah for instigating the conflict. So Al-Jazeera used historical events such as the Israeli invasions of Lebanon in 1978, 1982, 1984, 1993 and 1996 to persuade its viewers, especially the Arab youth generation, that Israel had had a hostile attitude towards Lebanon long before the inception of Hezbollah. Al-Jazeera here tried to intertextually contextualise the conflict by giving a historical account of previous conflicts in Lebanon which involved Israel. Some of these conflicts had devastating effects on the Lebanese society. Fairclough (1989: 155) places great importance on intertextuality in understanding existing meanings of texts, saying:

> The concept of intertextual context requires us to view discourses and texts from a historical perspective, in contrast with the more usual position in language studies which would regard a text as analysable without reference to other texts, in abstraction from its historical context. (Fairclough 1989: 155)

It is worth mentioning here that the term 'intertextuality' was used first by Julia Kristeva in her writing during the 1960s and early 1970s. Kristeva's notion of intertextuality was influenced by Bakhtin, who often complained of the neglect of establishing links between current texts and previous texts and considered each utterance to have traces of other utterances (Fairclough 1992b: 102). These utterances have their own meanings which are often reworked, adopted and often used by current speakers.

As will be demonstrated from our analysis of the three channels, there are some common discursive features that go back to the inception of the Arab media, but are used by Arabic channels in different forms to convey the meaning of contemporary events.

For instance, some of the channels alluded to the historical conflict between Israel and Lebanon, applying to it certain terminologies which were used during those conflicts.

Fairclough (1992b) refers to two types of intertextuality: manifest and constitutive. The former is explicitly marked in the text through the use of quotations, while the latter means 'the configuration of discourse conventions that go into its production' (Fairclough 1992b: 104). It is at times difficult to figure out the discourse convention when dealing with media texts, but an interpretation of the text in relation to the context and the process of production of this type of discourse can help decipher such a type of intertextuality.

Passive *v.* active

Al-Arabiya uses the active form in most of its headlines, where the agent of the action is clearly stated; however, when the action is related to killings and death, the channel uses the passive voice. Examples of this include '20 killed' and 'more than 40 civilians are killed'. In his analysis of Al-Arabiya's coverage of the war in Iraq, Al-Saggaf (2006) found that the channel reported the killing in the passive voice, without specifying those responsible. According to Fairclough (1989: 125), 'Agentless passive leaves causality and agency unclear'. In contrast, Al-Jazeera reported the killing in the active form, identifying the perpetrators: 'the Israeli military announces the killing of two members of Hezbollah', 'Hezbollah launches a missile' and 'the Israeli army commit a massacre'. As these examples demonstrate, Al-Jazeera was very explicit in stating the doer or agent responsible for the action on both sides.

Wading through Al-Jazeera's reports and news items, one cannot help noticing the excessive use of the active voice in them. Although the Arabic sentences are often verbal, that is, where preference is given to the verb, Al-Jazeera's headings are nominal sentences, where the subject precedes the verb. Nominalisation can be used to emphasise a noun or an action. Unlike Al-Arabiya, which removed the agent from its sentences in matters related to killings, Al-Jazeera placed the agent at the beginning of the sentence. Some might consider this part of Al-Jazeera's naming and shaming strategy; others may interpret it as part of its reporting strategy. In his analysis of the coverage of the same conflict by an American and an Iranian newspaper, *Newsweek* and *Kayhan*, respectively, Yaghoobi (2009) concluded that there were 'patterns of mystification of agency or actor of the process' by resorting to the passive or nominalisation. My findings, however, show completely different patterns. Both Al-Jazeera and Al-Arabiya resorted to the active form, where the agent is explicitly stated, but Al-Arabiya and Al-Hurra often used the passive in incidents of killings, for example '828 Lebanese civilians killed'. When Al-Hurra reported the displacement of civilians on both sides because of the conflict, however, it used the active voice when talking about the cause of the displacement of Israeli civilians:

A big number of Israeli civilians flee away their homes because of the missiles launched by Hezbollah.

In this report the agent or the doer of the action was clearly stated. The statement made it clear that Hezbollah had caused the displacement of civilians. When reporting the same stories from the Lebanese side, however, the channel resorted to the passive voice, such as the following:

Fleeing started after roads and cars were destroyed by the aerial strike. (August 2006)

As this example shows, the agent or doer of the action remained anonymous. The reporter could have used the 'Israeli aerial strike', but chose instead not to specify the agent in this case.

Theories of narratives of media discourse are often based on two main issues: the story and the presentation. The story is the accumulation of events and their sequence, but the presentation is related to the discourse and the way the story is put forward to the reader. This includes the choice of lexis and sentence structure (Fairclough 1995: 91). In his analysis of an editorial from *The Sun* newspaper about Saddam Hussein, Fairclough notes that the newspaper used the following collocation to describe Saddam: 'mad menace, tinpot tyrant, the Iraqi madman has pushed the West too far'. In his comments on the selection of this type of lexis,

Fairclough associates the term 'mad' with the discourse of madness, and 'menace' with the discourse of political extremism. The selection of this terminology could be seen to be ideologically motivated and politically calculated. 'Journalists don't only recount events, they also interpret and explain them, try to get people to see things and to act in certain ways, and aim to entertain' (Fairclough 1995: 91). I draw here on Fairclough's definition of ideology, which is the construction of reality 'built into various dimensions of the forms/meanings of discursive practices, and which contribute to the production, reproduction or transformation of relations of domination' (Fairclough 1992b: 87). Ideology can be reflected in language in different ways. It is a 'property' of both structure and events (Fairclough 1992b). As demonstrated above, the representation of discourse in Al-Jazeera, Al-Arabiya and Al-Hurra to some extent reflects their different ideologies, especially in reference to the selection of lexis.

Conclusion

This chapter has introduced the notion of discourse and demonstrated how Arabic channels have shown different approaches in the way they report conflicts. Such differences can be traced back to the changing Arabic political landscape and the role of the transnational media in promoting this new discourse. The competitive nature of these new media has produced a wide range of discourse genres. Some of these discourse genres reflect, though not entirely clearly, their ideological and political orientations. As the analysis shows, Al-Jazeera, Al-Arabiya and Al-Hurra have used different discourses to represent the content and meaning of the news. Al-Hurra and Al-Arabiya have shown some similarities in their coverage of the conflict, and this is manifested in their selection of lexis to represent different parties in the conflict. Both channels seem to cover the conflict, taking into account their sponsors' stance. Al-Jazeera's strategy is different. Its coverage of the conflict could be seen to be from an Arab perspective.

The results of the textual analysis demonstrated that the three channels have employed different strategies in reporting the conflict. The analysis has also confirmed that the three channels have different ideological orientations, which are clearly manifested in their discursive practices. These ideologies are often projected into the texts through the careful selection of lexis and representation of discourses. This reinforces Fowler's statement that 'news is not just a value-free reflection of facts. Anything that is said or written about the world is articulated from a particular ideological position' (1991: 101). Fowler's words were widely echoed by Gee (1999: 2) who said: 'When we speak or write we always take a particular perspective on what the world is like.' The power of language as a communicative tool and its impact on the reader cannot be underestimated. Language is 'an instrument of control as well as communication' (Kress and Hodge 1993: 6). As the analysis demonstrated, the difference in the usage of language in describing actions and groups has an impact on the reader, and thus changes his or her attitudes towards these groups. In Fowler's words 'newspapers in part adopt this language for their own end, in deploying it, reproduce the attitudes of the powerful' (1991: 23).

Conclusion

The Arab media has developed slowly since the independence of most Arab countries. Its development has been impeded by a variety of factors, some of which still exist. It may be said that audio-visual media has developed rapidly and gained popularity and recognition across the Arab world. Radio, in particular, was and is still the main source of news and information in most Arab countries. Radio's popularity can be traced to the high level of illiteracy that gripped the Arab world. Illiteracy had a great impact on the development of print media, as a high proportion of Arab people could not read or write, and newspapers were accessed only by those elite who could read both Arabic and other, foreign languages. The underdeveloped economy in most Arab countries also contributed to the slow development of print media because of the low level of readership in some Arabic countries. As efforts were exerted to improve literacy rates across the Arab world, however, the print media started expanding, and, as a result, there has been a proliferation of daily and weekly newspapers across the Arab world. The Arab public today enjoys a wide range of print media in different languages. In rural areas, however, there is still very slow progress in print media, as most of the people there are illiterate or financially cannot afford newspapers.

The interest in audio-visual media, though, has rocketed in almost every Arab country over the last decade or so. Almost every home has a television set or a radio. Television came relatively late to the Arab world, and at one time was confined to wealthy elite Arab families. As technology progressed, however, television has become a necessity in most Arab countries. Today, and because of competition and globalisation, the Arab public have access, not only to national television, but to some transnational channels. This is thanks to the proliferation of satellite channels in most Arab countries, which have not only enabled the Arab public to access international media, but have encouraged them to compare and contrast the information received on their state-run television with that disseminated via international and transnational media.

Traditionally, state media was run and controlled by the government. This media's attention centred on domestic issues such as the daily activities of governments, and international news and information hardly featured. The arrival of satellite channels and transnational Arab media changed the Arab media landscape, however, and the Arab public now has a free access to transnational Arab media that have emerged as very vocal and critical of Arab governments. The most striking point about the transnational media is the speed at which it has brought change to the Arab world. It has adopted a Western media outlook. The introduction of call-in shows has been seen as one of the first steps towards recognising the right of the Arab public to debate. These new platforms have not only encouraged the Arab public to debate issues of interest to them, but have given them a platform to air their concerns. The Arab public have seized the opportunity and got involved in all sorts of discussions, which could not be offered on the state media.

Some Arab governments have increasingly voiced concerns about this new media approach, which they argue constitutes a threat to the unity and security of the Arab states. Undeterred, channels like Al-Jazeera continue to engage the Arab public, and its popularity has rocketed. It has attracted both praise and criticism for its broadcasting. It has been praised for its bold move to offer free and transparent coverage of events regionally and internationally; but it has also attracted a cloud of criticism from Arab governments and leaders who feel the new range of Al-Jazeera threatens Arab unity and culture. Armed with its desire 'to promote freedom of expression' across the Arab world,

Al-Jazeera seems to shrug off the sharp criticism it has received from Arab governments; however, that criticism has grown louder and louder since the war on Afghanistan. Its coverage of the war was not to the taste of the American government, which complained about the channel's bias against the United States.

The launch of transnational Arab media has brought with it a sense of accountability and responsibility. The transnational Arab media have worked towards holding Arab governments accountable for their actions; however, the Arab media itself should be held accountable for its actions by the Arab public. Such actions include its failure to address human rights issues, freedom of expression, and support for the voiceless and opposition.

The international events that occurred over the last decade or so have strengthened the Arab media and led to the inception of new channels. The war on Iraq has been a turning point in the history of Arab media. The war not only contributed to the emergence of new channels, but encouraged a new genre of broadcasting. The competition between Al-Jazeera, Al-Arabiya and Al-Hurra has granted the Arab public access to information which was impossible to access before the launch of these channels. The inception of transnational channels reflects the genuine interest of some governments to communicate their policies to the Arab public, and where possible have some influence on them. As mentioned in Chapter 3, both Al-Hurra and Al-Arabiya were launched to rival Al-Jazeera, which has been accused of 'irresponsible and unbalanced' journalism. Al-Hurra and Radio Sawa were launched to improve and refine the United States's image in the Arab world, as well as to promote freedom and democracy to the Arab world. Al-Arabiya, on the other hand, was launched to provide a 'balanced' coverage in response to Al-Jazeera's coverage.

Such a diversity in the strategies of the three channels has enriched the Arab media landscape and brought with it new broadcasting standards that have been emulated by some state-run media. As a result, we have witnessed first-hand the relaxation of the codes of media operation in the Arab world. The diversity and multiplicity of the Arab media could be attributed to global competition. After September 11th, we saw the proliferation of international media directed at the Arab public. It could be argued that the inception of this international media has led some Arab media to be open and transparent in their broadcast. As a result, we have seen more open and transparent media, manifested, at least, in the transnational media. The global competition has put the Arab public at the centre of the Arab media's interest. The Arab public has become more valued, respected and defended by this new media. Interestingly enough, the Arab public has become part and parcel of the media operation, contributing to its programmes and evaluating its practices. It could be concluded that the transnational Arab media have empowered the Arab public, and turned it from a passive entity into an active one.

The change in the Arab media is clearly demonstrated in its type of discourse, which could be characterised as a liberal discourse. The new call-in shows have given the hitherto silent majority a voice to air their concerns and discontent. In addition to opening up platforms for the Arab public, the Arab media have adopted a discourse of empowerment and emancipation. But, what is striking about the analysis of the discourse of the three channels under examination is the big gulf in that discourse. The three channels adopted different discourse strategies in describing groups and actions in the 2006 Hezbollah–Israel conflict. Such a variation in the discourse is attributed to the different broadcasting strategies adopted by these channels. Their discourse shapes and is shaped by their ideological orientations. According to Fairclough and Wodak (1997: 258), 'discourse is socially constitutive as well as socially shaped: it constitutes situations, objects of knowledge, and the social identities of and relationships between people and groups of people.'

The analysis of the discursive practices of the three channels concludes that each has adopted a different strategy in reporting the conflict. The description of actions and groups differs widely from one channel to another. This variation in the selection of language reflects clearly the variation in the channels' strategies and policies. What is intriguing about these channels is that they all speak the same language and represent the same culture, so one would expect them to be homogeneous in their coverage of events, but their discursive practices reveal the opposite. The analysis of their coverage of the conflict reinforces the assumption that the Arab media has changed both in its outlook and in its practice. It also shows that the Arab public is no longer a hostage of one discourse, but has access to a variety of discourses that reflect different opinions and views. The change in discourse has engulfed not only the media, but the Arab public as well. As stated in Chapter 3, the Arab public have adopted a new discourse of empowerment and emancipation: a discourse governed by the notions of fairness and freedom. For the first time in its long history, the Arab public can use a discourse of accountability and reprimand against its governments.

Such a change is very revealing indeed. It reveals that both the Arab public and the media are moving in the same direction. It also shows that both media and Arab public have some impact on each other. This impact has been manifested in the successful way some transnational channels have mobilised the Arab public to take action in support of Palestinians and Iraqis. We have also seen how the active stance adopted by the Arab public has pushed some of the Arab media to take the public's side and, in some cases, adopt a critical approach against both regional and Western governments.

This book has shed more light on the development and diversity of the Arab media. The historical background is set to acquaint the reader with the nature and type of development the Arab media has undergone. The main factors that have impeded the early stages of development of the Arab media have also been examined. An insight into the past history of the Arab media has helped us to understand current Arab media broadcasting. The global and regional competition could be said to have contributed to the emergence of a new Arab media landscape. The transnational media have broken all taboos and crossed all red lines. In a summary, the new transnational media has introduced the Arab public to a new media culture: a culture of accountability, responsibility and respect of other opinions. Such achievements are very modest, however, when compared with the major achievements of the Western media.

With the emergence of new media such as Facebook and Twitter, one would envisage a radical change in the way information is selected and disseminated to the Arab public. The 2011 developments in Egypt, Tunisia and across the Arab world serve as a reminder that the new media cannot be controlled, and that the traditional means of monitoring and controlling the dissemination of information are no longer valid. Today, traditional media use new media as a new source for collecting news and information. The new media has not only changed the method of collecting, disseminating and receiving news and information, but it has also given the public the active role of contributing to the circulation of news. This new phenomenon requires that the traditional media in the Arab world review their way of operation. The emergence of the new media does not only constitute a challenge to the traditional media, but poses a challenge for governments across the Middle East. The likelihood of controlling the operation of this media is very slim. We have already witnessed how the Iranian government was unable to control the flow of information in and out of the country during the protest against the 2009 Iranian presidential election. One would envisage that Arab governments would review their media code of practice and allow more flux of information in and out of their states. The challenge that the new media poses is still in its infancy and will not have a big impact on the way information is disseminated across the Arab world. This is partly due to the fact that a large percentage of the Arab public has yet to have access to the new media and it is still confined to those elite who have both the skills and financial means to access it; however, with the growth of the Arab population and the spread of technology, especially in the Gulf States, it is expected that the Arab youth generation will have more access to the new media.

Notes

Chapter 1

[1] UAR–Saudi Relations. Background for dinner conversation with Faisal. 21 June 1966.

[2] www. Stanleyfoundation.org/articles, retrieved October 2010.

[3] Second inaugural address, 4 March 1805, online: http://cclce.org/files/ResourceCD/documents/USA/19th_century/1805_Thomas_Jefferson%27s_Second_Inaugural_Address.html.

Chapter 2

[1] 'And now, for the . . . in English from COVER STORY', *The Canberra Times*, 16 November 2006.

[2] 'We break 100 million barrier' (press release), Aljazeera.net, 4 October 2007, online: http://english.aljazeera.net/aboutus/2007/10/2008525184830438575.html.

[3] Ibid.

[4] http://islam-west.com/2007/10/cnn-dumped-for-al-jazeera-english-in.html.

[5] Ibid.

[6] http://www.guardian.co.uk/media/2008/jan/30/tvnews.television.

Chapter 3

[1] *Al-Quds Al-Arabi*, editorial, 17 February 2004, p. 1.

[2] Rugh, William (2004), comments on Radio Sawa and Al-Hurra television.

[3] 'Al-Hurra's programming policies and procedures', report number ISP-IB-08-45, May 2008, Arlington, VA: United States Department of State and the Broadcasting Board of Governors, Office of Inspector General.

Chapter 4

[1] See, for example, articles by Dev Raj Dahal on the *Nepal Democracy* website: http://www.nepaldemocracy.org.

[2] Ibid.

Bibliography

Abd al-Rahman, A. (1996), *Al-Sihafah al-Arabiyah fi muwajahat al-tabaiyah wa-al-ikhtiraq al-Sihyuni*, Saffat: Dar al-Fikr al-Arabi.

Abunimah, A. and H. Ibish (2001), 'The CNN of the Arab world deserves our respect', *Los Angeles Times*, 22 October 2001, online: http://www.latimes.com/new/opinion/la-10220libich.story.

Adams, G. (2006), 'Do not adjust your sets: an alternative view of the world', *The Independent*, 15 November 2006, online: http://www.independent.co.uk/news/media/do-not-adjust-your-sets-an-alternative-view-of-the-world-424334.html.

Adams, M. (2006), 'Hybridizing habitus and reflexivity: towards an understanding of contemporary identity?', *Sociology*, 40(3): 511–28.

Al-Hail, A. (2000), 'The age of new media: the role of Al-Jazeera satellite TV in developing aspects of civil society in Qatar', *Transnational Broadcasting Studies*, 4, online: http://www.tbsjournal.com/Archives/Spring00/Articles4/Ali/Al-Hail/al-hail.html.

Al-Homayed, T. (2004), 'Al-Hurra channel . . . Washington's error', *Arab News*, 16 July 2004, online: http://archive.arabnews.com/?page=7&section=0&article=48414&d=16&m=7&y=2004.

Al-Saggaf, Y. (2006), 'The online public sphere in the Arab world: the war in Iraq on the Al Arabiya website', *Journal of Computer-Mediated Communication*, 12(1), online: http://jcmc.indiana.edu/vol12/issue1/al-saggaf.html.

Amin, H. (1995), 'Who is watching what? Arab state broadcasting and audience profile', paper presented at the Twentieth Annual Symposium, Center for Contemporary Arab Studies, School of Foreign Services, Washington, DC, 20–1 April.

Amin, H. (2001), 'Mass media in the Arab states between diversification and stagnation: an overview', in Kai Hafez (ed.), *Mass Media, Politics, and Society in the Middle East*, Cresskill, NJ: Hampton Press, pp. 23–44.

Amin, H. (2002), 'Freedom as a value in Arab media: perceptions and attitudes among journalists', *Political Communication*, 19: 125–35.

Amin, H. (2004), 'Social engineering: transnational broadcasting and its impact on peace in the Middle East', *Global Media Journal*, 3(4), online: http://lass.calumet.purdue.edu/cca/gmj/sp05/sp04/gmj-sp04-amin.htm.

Anderson, J. (1997), 'Globalizing politics and religion in the Muslim world', *The Journal of Electronic Publishing*, 3(1).

Arrabyee, N. (2009), 'Al-Arabiya criticized and Al-Jazeera praised over Gaza war coverage', *Yemen Observer*, 5 January 2009, online: http://www.yobserver.com/front-page/10015493.html.

Atton, C. (2002), *Alternative Media*. London: SAGE Publications.

Atton, C. (2002b), 'News culture and new social movements: radical journalism and the mainstream media', *Journalism Studies*, 3(4): 491–505.

Awatef, A. (1996), *The Arab Press: Confronting Dependency and Zionist Penetration*, (in Arabic), Cairo: Dar Al-Fiqr Al-Arabi.

Ayish, M. (1991), 'Foreign voices as people's choices: BBC popularity in the Arab world', *Middle Eastern Studies*, 27(3): 374–88.

Ayish, M. (2001a), 'The changing face of Arab communications: media survival in the information age', in Kai Hafez (ed.), *Mass Media, Politics, and Society in the Middle East*, Cresskill, NJ: Hampton Press, pp. 111–36.

Ayish, M. (2001b), 'American-style journalism and Arab world television: an exploratory study of news selection at six Arab world satellite television channels', *Transnational Broadcasting Studies*, 6, online: http://www.tbsjournal.com/Archives/Spring01/Ayish.html.

Ayish, M. (2005), 'Media brinkmanship in the Arab world', in Mohamed Zayani (ed.), *The Al Jazeera Phenomenon. Critical Perspectives on New Arab Media*, New York: Pluto Press, pp. 106–26.

Azet, M. F. M. (1992), *News Agencies in the Arab World. The Sun Rises for Publication, Distribution and Print*, (in Arabic), Jidda: Dar Al-Shuruk.

Azran, T. (2004), 'Resisting peripheral exports: Al Jazeera's war images on US television', *Media International Australia incorporating Culture & Policy*, 113: 75–86.

Azzi, A. (1998), 'Mass media in the Grand Maghrib: Morocco – Algeria – Tunisia', *ReoCities*, 11 June 1998, online: http://www.reocities.com/Athens/ithaca/8257/maghrib.htm.

Bahry, L. Y. (2001), 'The new Arab media phenomenon: Qatar's Al-Jazeera', *Middle East Policy*, 8(2): 88–99.

Barker, C. (2000), *Cultural Studies: Theory and Practice*, London: SAGE Publications.

Barkho, L. (2006), 'The Arabic Aljazeera vs Britain's BBC and America's CNN: Who does journalism right?', *American Communication Journal*, 8(1): 1–15.

Bell, A. (1991), *The Language of News Media*, Oxford: Blackwell.

Bessaiso, E. (2005), 'Al-Jazeera and the war in Afghanistan: a delivery system or mouthpiece?', in Mohamed Zayani (ed.), *The Al-Jazeera Phenomenon. Critical Perspectives on New Arab Media*, New York: Pluto Press.

Bourdieu, P. (1977), *Outline of a Theory of Practice*, Cambridge: Cambridge University Press.

Bourdieu, P. (1988), *Homo Academicus*, trans. Peter Collier, Cambridge: Polity Press.

Boyd, D. A. (ed.) (1993), *Broadcasting in the Arab World: A Survey of the Electronic Media in the Middle East*, 2nd edn, Ames, IA: Iowa State University Press.

Boyd, D. and Hussein A. (1993), 'The impact of the home video cassette recorder on Egyptian film and television consumption patterns', *The European Journal of Communication*, 18(1): 77–87.

Brown, G. and G. Yule (1983), *Discourse Analysis*, Cambridge: Cambridge University Press.

Burstein, N. (2007), 'HOT cable to drop CNN for Al-Jazeera', *The Jerusalem Post*, 23 October 2007, online: https://desertpeace.wordpress.com/2007/10/23/al-jazeeras-english-channel-comes-to-israel/.

Candlin, S. (1997), 'An analysis of the discourse of nurses and patients in the context of health assessment', unpublished PhD thesis, Lancaster: Lancaster University.

Chafe, W. (1992), 'The flow of ideas in a sample of written language', in William C. Mann and Sandra A. Thompson (eds), *Discourse Description: Diverse Linguistic Analyses of a Fund-raising Text*, Amsterdam: John Benjamins, 267ff.

Chafe, W. [1996] (2003), 'Consciousness and language', in Jef Verschueren, Jan-Ola Östman, Jan Blommaert and Chris Bulcaen (eds.), *Handbook of Pragmatics Online*, Amsterdam: John Benjamins.

Cochrane, P. (2007), 'Saudi Arabia's media influence', *Journal of Arab Media and Society*, 3, online: http://www.arabmediasociety.com/?article=421.

Coleman, S. and K. Ross (2010), *The Media and the Public: Them and Us in Media Discourse*, Oxford: Blackwell.

Conniff, B. (2010), ' Al-Hurra: today, tomorrow and beyond', *Perspectives*, II(10), online: http://www.layalina.tv/Publications/Perspectives/BrianConniff.html.

Davis, K. (1988), *Power Under the Microscope: Toward a Grounded Theory of Gender Relations in Medical Encounters*. Dordrecht: Foris.

Dickinson, Lieutenant Colonel J. H., United States Army (2005), *A Strategy to Improve a Negative American Image in the Middle East*, 18 March 2005, US Army War College, Carlisle, PA.

Downing, J. D. H. (2003), 'Audiences and readers of alternative media: the absent lure of the virtually unknown', *Journal of Media, Culture and Society*, 25: 625–45.

El-Nawawy, M. (2006), 'U S public diplomacy in the Arab world: the news credibility of Radio Sawa and Television Alhurra in five countries', *Journal of Global Media and Communication*, 2(2): 183–203.

El-Nawawy, Mohamed and Adel Iskandar (2002), *Al-Jazeera: How the Free Arab News Network Scooped the World and Changed the Middle East*. Boulder, CO: Westview Press.

Entman, R. M. (1993), 'Framing toward a clarification of a fractured paradigm', *Journal of Communication*, 43(4): 51–8.

Ermes, A. (2004), 'The Arab media in Britain', 7 July 2004, online: http:// www.Aliomarermes.co.uk/resources/view_article.cfm.

Essoulami, S. (2006), 'The press in the Arab world: 100 years of suppressed freedom', online: http://www.al-bab.com/media/introduction. htm.

Exum, A. (2006), 'Interview with Brigadier General Mark T. Kimmitt, Deputy Director for Strategy and Plans, US Central Command', *Transnational Broadcasting Studies*, 16, online: http://www.tbsjournal.com/ KimmittInterview.html/.

Fairclough, N. (1989), *Language and Power*, London: Longman.

Fairclough, N. (1992a), *Critical Language Awareness*, London: Longman.

Fairclough, N. (1992b), *Discourse and Social Change*, Cambridge: Polity Press.

Fairclough, N. (1993), 'Critical discourse analysis and the marketization of public discourse: the universities', *Discourse and Society*, 4(2): 133–68.

Fairclough, N. (1994), 'Conversationalization of public discourse and the authority of the consumer', in R. Keat, N. Whiteley and N. Abercrombie (eds), *The Authority of the Consumer*, London: Routledge, pp. 253–68.

Fairclough, N. (1995), *Media Discourse*, London: Arnold.

Fairclough, N. (1996), 'Border crossings: discourse and social change in contemporary societies', in Hywel Coleman and Lynne Cameron (eds), *Change and Language*, Clevedon: British Association for Applied Lingusitics in Association with Multilingual Matters, pp. 3–17.

Fairclough, N. (2001), *Language and Power*, 2nd edn, Harlow: Pearson Education.

Fairclough, N. and R. Wodak (1997), 'Critical Discourse Analysis', in T. A. van Dijk (1997) *Discourse as Social Interaction*, vol. 2, London: SAGE Publications, pp. 258–84.

Feuilherade, P. (2003), 'Al Jazeera competitor launches', *BBC News*, 20 February 2003, online: http://news.bbc.co.uk/1/hi/world/middle_ east/ 2780985.stm.

Fiss, P. C. and P. Mirsch (2005), 'The discourse of globalization: framing and sense-making of an emerging concept', *American Sociological Review*, 70(1): 29–52.

Foucault, M. (1972), *The Archaeology of Knowledge*, trans Alan Sheridan, New York: Pantheon.

Foucault, M. (1977), *Language Counter-Memory, Practice*, trans. D. Bouchard, New York: Harper and Row.

Foucault, M. (1981), *History of Sexuality*, vol.1, Harmondsworth: Penguin Books.

Fowler, R. (1991), 'Critical linguistics', in Kirsten Malmkjaer (ed.), *Linguistic Encyclopedia*, London and New York: Routledge, pp. 89–95.

Fowler, R. (1996), *Linguistic Criticism*, 2nd edn, Oxford: Oxford University Press.

Fowler, R., B. Hodge, G. Kress and T. Trew, T. (1979), *Language and Control*, London: Routledge and Kegan Paul.

Fraser, Nancy (1992), 'Rethinking the public sphere', in Craig Calhoun (ed.), *Habermas and the Public Sphere*, Cambridge, MA: MIT Press, pp. 109–42.

Friedman, T. (2001), 'Foreign affairs; Glasnost in the Gulf', *The New York Times*, 27 February, online: http://query.nytimes.com/gst/fullpage.html?res=9E01E4D91F39F934A15751C0A9679C8B63.

Gee, J. P. (1999), *An Introduction to Discourse Analysis Theory and Method*, 2nd edn, New York: Routledge.

Glass, D. (2001), 'The global flow of information: a critical appraisal from the perspective of Arab-Islamic information sciences', in Kai Hafez (ed.), *Mass Media, Politics, and Society in the Middle East*, Cresskill, NJ: Hampton Press, pp 217–40.

Goffman, E. (1974), *Frame Analysis*, New York: Harper Colophon Books.

Habermas, J. (1984), *Theory of Communicative Action*, vol. 1, trans. T. McCarthy, London: Heinemann.

Habermas, J. ([1962] 1989), *The Structural Transformation of the Public Sphere*, Cambridge, MA: MIT Press.

Hafez, K. (2007), *The Myth of Media Globalisation*, Cambridge: Polity Press.

Hahn, O. (2007), 'Culture of TV news journalism and prospects for a transcultural public sphere', in Naomi Sakr (ed.), *Arab Media and Political Renewal: Community, Legitimacy and Public Life*, London and New York: I. B. Tauris.

Hall, S. (1997), 'The spectacle of the "other"', in S. Hall (ed.), *Representation: Cultural Representations and Signifying Practices*, London: SAGE Publications, pp. 223–79.

Halliday, M. A. K. (1973), *Explorations in the Function of Language*, London: Edward Arnold.

Halliday, M. A. K. (1975), *Learning How to Mean*, London: Edward Arnold.

Halliday, M. A. K. (1978), *Language as a Social Semiotic*, London: Edward Arnold.

Halliday, M. A. K. and R. Hasan (1976), *Cohesion in English*, London: Longman.

Halliday, M. A. K. and R. Hasan (1989), *Language, Context, and Text: Aspects of Language in a Social-Semiotic Perspective*, Oxford: Oxford University Press.

Hammond, A. (2007), 'Saudi Arabia's media empire: keeping the masses at home', *Journal of Arab Media and Society*, 3, online: http://www.arabmediasociety.com/?article=420.

Hartley, J. (1996), *Popular Reality: Journalism, Modernity, Popular Culture*. London: Edward Arnold.

Hegasy, S. (1997), *Staat, Öffentlichkeit und Zivilgesellschaft in Marokko*, Hamburg: Deutsches Orient Institut.

Heil, A. (2006), 'America's Vanishing Voice?', *Transnational Broadcasting Studies*, 16, online: http://www.tbsjournal.com/Heil.html.

Hjarvard, S. (ed.) (2001), *News in a Globalized Society*, Gothenburg: Nordicom.

Hodge, R. and G. Kress (1993), *Language as Ideology*, 2nd edn, London: Routledge.

Hodges, L. W. (1986), 'Defining press responsibility: a functional approach', in D. Elliott (ed.), *Responsible Journalism*, Newbury Park, CA: SAGE Publications, pp. 13–31.

Hofheinz, A. (2007), 'Arab internet use: popular trends and public impact', in Naomi Sakr (ed.), *Arab Media and Political Renewal: Community, Legitimacy and Public Life*, London and New York: I. B. Tauris, pp. 56–78, 178–84.

Holmwood, L. (2008), 'Al-Jazeera English in "staffing crisis"', *The Guardian*, 30 January 2008, online: http://www.guardian.co.uk/media/2008/jan/30/tvnews.television.

Human Rights Watch (2005), *False Freedom: Online Censorship in the Middle East and North Africa*, 15 November, E1710, online: http://www.unhcr.org/refworld/docid/45cc445f2.html.

Ibahrine, M. (2002), 'Democratisation and the press: the case of Morocco', *Nord-Süd Aktuell*, 4: 632–40.

Iskandar, A. (2006), 'Is Al Jazeera alternative? Mainstreaming alterity and assimilating discourses of dissent', *Transnational Broadcasting Studies*, 16, online: http://www.tbsjournal.com/Iskandar.html.

James, L. (2006), 'Whose voice? Nasser, the Arabs, and "Sawt al-Arab" Radio'. *Transnational Broadcasting Studies*, 16, online: http://www.tbsjournal.com/James.html.

Jarrah, N. (2008), 'The rise and decline of London as a pan-Arab media hub', *Journal of Arab Media and Society*, 4, online: http://www.arab mediasociety.com/index.php?article=571&p=0.

Jusiæ, T. (2009), 'Media discourse and the politics of ethnic conflict: the case of Yugoslavia', in P. Kolstø (ed.), *Media Discourse and the Yugoslav Conflicts: Representations of Self and Other*, Aldershot and Burlington, VT: Ashgate Publishing.

Kamalipour, Y. R. and H. Mowlana (eds) (1994), *Mass Media in the Middle East: A Comprehensive Handbook*, Westport, CT: Greenwood Press.

Karaiskou, A. (2007), 'Al-Jazeera after 9/11: the emergence of an Arab world-class news organization', *Center for Mediterranean & Middle Eastern Studies*, 6: 2–4.

Khatib, L. (2007), 'Television and public action in Beirut spring', in Naomi Sakr (ed.), *Arab Media and Political Renewal: Community, Legitimacy and Public Life*, London and New York: I. B. Tauris.

Kirchner, H. (2001), 'Internet in the Arab world: a step towards "information society"?', in in Kai Hafez (ed.), *Mass Media, Politics, and Society in the Middle East*, Cresskill, NJ: Hampton Press, pp. 137–59.

Kraidy, M. (2002), 'Hybridity in cultural globalization', *Communication Theory*, 12(3): 316–39.

Kraidy, M. (2005), 'Reality television and politics in the Arab world: preliminary observations', *Transnational Broadcasting Studies*, 15, online: http://www.tbsjournal.com/Archives/Fall05/Kraidy.html.

Kraidy, M. (2007), *Global Media Studies*. New York: Taylor and Francis.

Kraidy, M. and J. F. Khalil (2009), *Arab Television Industries*, London: Palgrave Macmillan.

Kress, G. and R. Hodge (1979), *Language as Ideology*, London: Routledge.

Kress, G. and R. Hodge (1988), *Social Semiotics*, Cambridge: Polity Press.

Lahlali, M. (2007), *Critical Discourse Analysis and Classroom Discourse Practices*, Munich: Lincom Europa.

Lahlali, M. (2009), 'Alternative Arab media and the right to communicate in the Middle East', In Aliaa Dakroury, Mahmoud Eid and Yahya R. Kamalipour (eds), *The Right to Communicate: Historical Hopes, Global Debates and Future Premises*, Dubuque, IA: Kendall Hunt.

Leudar, I., V. Marsland and J. Nekvapil (2004), 'On membership categorization: "us", "them" and "doing violence" in political discourse', *Discourse and Society*, 15(2–3): 243–66.

Levitt, T. (1983), 'The globalization of markets', *Harvard Business Review*, 61(3): 92–102.

Lynch, M. (2004), 'America and the Arab media environment', in William Rugh (ed.), *Engaging the Arab and Islamic Worlds Through Public Diplomacy: A Report and Action Recommendations*, Washington, DC: Public Diplomacy Council, pp. 90–108.

Lynch, M. (2006), *Voices of the New Arab Public: Iraq, Al-Jazeera, and Middle East Politics Today*, New York: Columbia University Press.

McQuail, D. (1994), *Mass Communication: an Introduction*, 3rd edn, London, Thousand Oaks, CA, and New Delhi: SAGE Publications.

Maddy-Weitzman, B. (2001), 'Contested Identities: Berbers, 'Berberism' and the State in North Africa', *The Journal of North African Studies*, 6(3): 23–47.

Mantzikos, I. V. (2007), 'The Issue of Press Freedom', *Center for Mediterranean & Middle Eastern Studies*, 6: 14–15.

Markovic, Z. M. (1997), *Benefits from the Enemy*, Belgrave: Agency Argument.

Martin, H.-P. and H. Schumann (1997), *The Global Trap: Globalization and the Assault on Prosperity and Democracy*, London and New York: Zed Books.

Mejcher, H. (2004), 'King Faisal Ibn Abdul Aziz Al Saud in the arena of world politics: a glimpse from Washington. 1950 to 1971', *British Journal of Middle Eastern Studies*, 31(1), 5–23.

Mellor, N. (2007), *Modern Arab Journalism: Problems and Prospects*, Edinburgh: Edinburgh University Press.

Merskin, D. (2004), 'The construction of Arabs as enemies: post-September 11 discourse of George W. Bush', *Mass Communication and Society*, 7(2): 157–75.

Mumby, K. D and R. P. Claire (1996), 'Organizational discourse', in T. A. van Dijk (1997) *Discourse as Social Interaction*, vol. 2, London: SAGE Publications, pp. 181–203.

Ohmae, K. (1990), *The Borderless World*, London: HarperCollins.

Pattiz, N. (2004), 'Radio Sawa and Alhurra TV: opening channels of mass communication in the Middle East', in William Rugh (ed.), *Engaging the Arab and Islamic Worlds Through Public Diplomacy: A Report and Action Recommendations*, Washington, DC: Public Diplomacy Council, pp. 156–9.

Pintak, L. (2006), 'Al-Jazeera International. A CNN for the developing world', *Speigel Online*, 16 November, online: http://www.spiegel.de/international/0,1518,448830,00.html.

Plaisance, P. L. (2000), 'The concept of media accountability reconsidered', *Journal of Mass Media Ethics*, 15(4): 257–68.

Poster, M. (2001), 'Citizens, digital media and globalization', *Mots Pluriels*, 18, online: http://www.arts.uwa.edu.au/MotsPluriels/MP1801mp.html.

Price, M. E. (1995), *Television: The Public Sphere and National Identity*, Oxford: Clarendon Press.

Robinson, D. (2005), 'Broadcast officials defend US-funded Arab televi-

sion', *Payvand Iran News*, 11 November 2005, online: http://www.pay
vand.com/news/05/nov/1100.html.

Rugh, W. (1979), *The Arab Press: News Media and Political Process in the Arab World*, Syracuse, NY: Syracuse University Press.

Rugh, W. A. (1987), *The Arab Press: News Media and Political Process in the Arab World*, 2nd edn, Syracuse, NY: Syracuse University Press.

Rugh, W. (2004), *Arab Mass Media: Newspapers, Radio, and Television in Arab Politics*, Westport, CT: Praeger.

Rugh, W. (2006), 'Anti-Americanism on Arab television: some outsider observations', *Transnational Broadcasting Studies*, 15, online: http://www.tbsjournal.com/Archives/Fall05/Rugh.html.

Rugh, W. A. (2007), 'Do National Political Systems Still Influence Arab Media?', *Arab Media and Society*, 2, online: http://arabmediasociety.sqgd.co.uk/topics/index.php?t_article=143.

Rugh, W. (2009), 'Repairing American public diplomacy', *Arab Media and Society*, 7, online: http://www.arabmediasociety.com/?article=709.

Sabry, T. (2005), 'What is global about Arab media?', *Global Media and Communication*, 1(1): 41–6.

Saghieh, H. (2004), 'Al-Jazeera: the world through Arab eyes', *openDemocracy*, 16 June 2004, online: http://www.opendemocracy.net/conflict-iraqivoices/article_1958.jsp.

Sakr, N. (2001), *Satellite Realms: Transnational Television, Globalization and the Middle East*, London and New York: I. B. Tauris.

Sakr, N. (ed.) (2007), *Arab Media and Political Renewal: Community, Legitimacy and Public Life*, London and New York: I. B. Tauris.

Sawant, P. B. (2003), 'Accountability in journalism', *Journal of Mass Media Ethics*, 18(1): 16–28.

Schleifer, A. (2006), 'The impact of Arab satellite television on prospects for democracy in the Arab world', *Transnational Broadcasting Studies*, 15, online: http://www.tbsjournal.com/Archives/Fall05/Schleifer.html.

Shummo, A. M. (1977), 'The right to communicate as seen in developing countries', abstracted from L. S. Harms and Jim Richstad (eds), *Evolving Perspectives on the Right to Communicate*, Honolulu: East West Center, pp. 247–55, online: http://www.righttocommunicate.org/viewDocument.atm?sectionName=summaries&id=50.

Silverstone, R. (1985), *Framing Science: The Making of a BBC Documentary*, London: BFI Publishing.

Snow, N. (2010), 'Alhurra to Al Youm: the maturation of U.S. television broadcasting in the Middle East', Syracuse, NY: Syracuse University, online: http://sites.maxwell.syr.edu/luce/snow.html.

Snyder, A. (2005), 'Al Hurra's struggle for legitimacy', *Jordan Times*,

1 December 2005, online: http://www.menafn.com/qn_news_story_
s.asp?StoryId=116426.

Sullivan, S. (2001), 'Courting Al-Jazeera, the sequel: estrangement
and signs of reconciliation', *Transnational Broadcasting Studies*, 7,
online: http://www.tbsjournal.com/Archives/Fall01/Jazeera_special.
htm.

Tafasca, A. (1984), 'Kanawat Al Itisal fi Al Maghrib', *Report*, Rabat, p. 11.

Tassopoulos, T. (2007), 'Media freedom. The role of the state in the Arab
world', *Center for Mediterranean & Middle Eastern Studies*, 6: 8–10.

Taweela, W. (2002), 'New media in the Arab world: the social and cultural
aspect', trans Lina Abu Nuwar, online: http://www.mafhoum.com/
press4/124S30.htm.

Toolan, M (1997), 'What is critical discourse analysis and why are
people saying such terrible things about it?', *Language and Literature*,
6(2): 83–103.

Tettey, W. (2001), 'The media and democratization in Africa: contribu-
tions, constraints and concerns of the private press', *Media, Culture and
Society*, 23(1): 5–31.

The Economist (2001), 'Al Jazeera: explosive matchbox,' 11 October, online:
http://www.economist.com/node/814185.

United Nations (1948), *The Universal Declaration of Human Rights*, New
York: United Nations, online: http://www.un.org/en/documents/
udhr/index.shtml.

van Dijk, T. (1988), *News as Discourse*, Hillsdale, NJ: Erlbaum.

van Dijk, T. A. (1991), *Racism in the Press*, London: Routledge.

van Dijk, T. A. (1995), 'Discourse semantics and ideology', *Discourse and
Society*, 6: 243–89.

van Dijk, T. A. (1996), 'Discourse as interaction in society', in T. A. van
Dijk (ed.), *Discourse as Social Interaction*, London: SAGE Publications,
vol. 2, pp. 1–37.

van Dijk, T. A. (ed.) (1997), *Discourse Studies: A Multidisciplinary Introduction*, 2 vols, London: SAGE Publications.

van Dijk, T. (1998), *Ideology: A Multidisciplinary Approach*, London: SAGE
Publications.

van Dijk, T. (2000), 'New(s) racism: a discourse analytical approach', in
Simon Cottle (ed.), *Ethnic Minorities and the Media*, Buckingham and
Philadelphia, PA: Open University Press, pp. 33–49.

van Dijk, T.A. (2006), 'Ideology and discourse analysis', *Journal of Political
Ideologies*, 11(2): 115–140.

Vogt, A. (2002), 'Regulation and self-regulation: the role of media com-
missions and professional bodies in the Muslim world', *Political Communication*, 19: 211–23.

Bibliography

Waheed, T. (2002), 'New media in the Arab world: the social and cultural impact', paper presented at the conference on New Media and Change in the Arab World, Amman, Jordan, 1 March 2002.

Widdowson, H. G. (1995), 'Discourse analysis: a critical view', *Language and Literature*, 11(2): 153–60.

Widdowson, H. G. (1996), 'Reply to Fairclough: discourse and interpretation: conjectures and refutations', *Language and Literature*, 5(1): 57–69.

Widdowson, H. G. (1998), 'The theory and practice of critical discourse analysis', *Journal of Applied Linguistics*, 19(1): 136–51.

Widdowson, H. G. (2004), *Text, Context, and Pretext: Critical Issues in Discourse Analysis*, Oxford: Blackwell.

Wise, L. (2005), 'A second look at Alhurra: US-funded channel comes of age on the front lines of the "battle for hearts and minds" ', *Transnational Broadcasting Studies*, 14, online: http://www.tbsjournal.com/Archives/Spring05/wise.htm.

Yaghoobi, M. (2009), 'A critical discourse analysis of the selected Iranian and American printed media on the representation of Hizbullah–Israel war', *Journal of Intercultural Communication*, 21, online: http://www.immi.se/intercultural/nr21/yaghoobi.htm.

Youmans, W. (2009), 'The war on ideas: Alhurra and US international broadcasting law in the "War on Terror"', *Westminster Papers in Communication and Culture*, 6(1): 45–68, online: http://westminsteruni.dev.squiz.co.uk/__data/assets/pdf_file/0010/19990/WPCC-Vol6-No1-William_Youmans.pdf.

Zaharana, R. S. (2005), 'Al Jazeera and American public diplomacy: a dance of intercultural (mis)communication', in Mohamed Zayani (ed.), *The Al Jazeera Phenomenon. Critical Perspectives on New Arab Media*, New York: Pluto Press.

Zayani, M. (ed.) (2005), *The Al Jazeera Phenomenon. Critical Perspectives on New Arab Media*, New York: Pluto Press.

Zayani, M. and M. Ayish (2006), 'Arab satellite television and crisis reporting: covering the fall of Baghdad', *International Communication Gazette*, 68: 473.

Zayani, M. (2007), 'Arab media, corporate communications, and public relations: the case of Al-Jazeera', *Asian Journal of Communication*, 18(3): 207–22.

Zayani, M. and S. Sahraoui (2007), *The Culture of Al Jazeera: Inside an Arab Media Giant*, Jefferson, NC: McFarland.

Zidan, S. M. H. (2006), 'Representation of viewpoint in opinion discourse. A comparative linguistic investigation of Arabic and British newspapers at time of conflict', PhD thesis, Leeds: University of Leeds.

Index

Other books by El Mustapha Lahlali

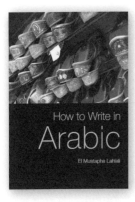

How to Write in Arabic

Aimed at intermediate level learners, this book explains the structure of Arabic sentences and paragraphs, providing a variety of phrases and idiomatic expressions for use in writing

2009 • 200pp
Pb 978 0 7486 3588 7 • £19.99
Hb 978 0 7486 3587 0 • £65.00

Advanced Media Arabic

Provides a variety of media texts and audio materials to help develop language, translation and analytical skills

2008 • 224pp
Pb 978 0 7486 3273 2 • £24.99
Hb 978 0 7486 3272 5 • £70.00

Essential Middle Eastern Vocabularies

Series Editor: Elisabeth Kendall

www.euppublishing.com/seres/EMEV

Short, accessible guides with key terms, up-to-date expressions, jargon and new coinages to express modern concepts across broad areas of interest such as the media, the internet, law and business.

KEY FEATURES:

- Terms grouped in thematic sections
- Easy-to-learn lists to test translation
- CD of audio podcasts to help check pronunciation
- Interactive audio e-flashcards

FORTHCOMING TITLES:

Media Persian

Dominic Parviz Brookshaw

July 2011 • 128pp
Pb 978 0 7486 4100 0 • £12.99
Hb 978 0 7486 4101 7 • £50.00

Media Arabic
2ND EDITION

Elisabeth Kendall

January 2012 • 128pp
Pb 978 0 7486 4495 7 • £12.99
Hb 978 0 7486 4499 7 • £50.00

Internet Arabic

Mourad Diouri

This short, accessible vocabulary provides ready-made lists of key terms and concepts in internet Arabic for translating both from and into Arabic.

DIVIDED INTO 11 KEY AREAS:

- General Terminology
- Web Browsing
- Written Online Communication
- Audio-Visual Online Communication
- Searching for Information on the Web
- E-Learning
- Online Social Networking
- Netiquette
- Online Security
- Internet Services
- My Digital Identity

January 2012 • 128pp
Pb 978 0 7486 4491 9 • £12.99
Hb 978 0 7486 4492 6 • £50.00